MW01248959

ISBN: 84-96492-15-X
Legal Deposit: M-5486-2006

The Bible of BRAZILIAN
Jiu Jitsu

柔術

Francisco Mansur 9th Dan
Kioto Jiu Jitsu System

Prolog

It is an honor for me to be able to publish this Grand Master and gentleman of the Martial Arts, whose name is Francisco Mansur. He has honored me by asking me to write the prolog of his first book, and this is especially true because he could very well have invited any one of the big names in the sector to present him. Mansur is a contemporary and historical reference in Brazilian Jiu-Jitsu. He lived the epic times of Jiu-Jitsu along with Helio Gracie, his Master, and from his gymnasiums in New York and Rio de Janeiro, he prepares and trains the future generations of the Soft Art.

The peculiarity that distinguishes him (apart from being one of the two 9th Degree black-belts active in the world in this style) is the results of his unquestionable teaching expertise. Mansur has structured and developed the entire system that he received from his Master, and we have to recognize that in principle, and despite what their flag says ("Order and Progress"), the average Brazilian, as with all inhabitants of warm countries, is not exactly a great lover of structure. Mansur has begun an enormous project with this book, a project that organizes the learning of the Jiu-Jitsu techniques in a succession of attacks and defenses that he arranges by chapters and subjects. In this first book (which we hope to be the first in a long series), readers, students, and the curious about Jiu-Jitsu will be able to study the basics in order to become true experts starting from zero. Everything in it has been thought out in order to facilitate the learning process. The angles of the shots have been carefully chosen in the photo series, and when the very execution of the movement hides the action, it has been complemented with a shot from the most advantageous angle. This has been signaled with the symbol of an old-fashioned camera and in this way indicating the direction from which the shot is explained. On occasion, the Master wanted to highlight the key to a certain movement and for that we have done a blow-up of the detail in question, normally enclosed in a circular space and/or with an attention sign.

It has been an arduous task that we have strived for hand in hand. To prepare this book, we lived together for two weeks, which consolidated a strong friendship that was felt from the first moment. The knowledge, the detail, and the attention with which the whole project has been elaborated by the Master will make this book a classic and a definitive reference for all lovers of Brazilian Jiu-Jitsu.

Alfredo Tucci,
Managing Director of Budo International
Budo International Publishing Co.

THE JIU-JITSU BIBLE

Why the JIU-JITSU BIBLE?

Because this book is going to show the authentic science of Jiu-Jitsu, its intrinsic and extrinsic usefulness, its true origin, its past, its present, and its glorious future.

God willing, it will take its rightful place as an Olympic sport.

Now you have in your hands the first volume of the collection of the KIOTO SYTEM OF BRAZILIAN JIU-JITSU, created in 1965 after ten years of study and practice by the Grand Master Francisco Mansur, who has the honor and pride of having been granted black belt by the Grand Master Helio Gracie, apart from being one of the six men in the world with a 9th Degree Red Belt from the Brazilian Jiu-Jitsu Confederation and from the International Brazilian Jiu-Jitsu Federation. He also currently occupies the charge of President of the New York State Brazilian Jiu-Jitsu Federation and is director of the International Confederation of Police & Security. Expert and author, as well as technician of this system—which has been perfected from its creation day after day for 40 years—you now have the unique opportunity to study with this master who has already given classes to roughly 20,000 students of both sexes and ages varying from 4 to 80. Make good use of it.

The movements of this SYSTEM follow a diverse methodology which works the reflexes, emotional control, and intelligence progressively.

The study and practice of this System has been consistently recommended by doctors, psychologists, and teachers for being a complete activity in the process of education that stimulates and/or develops:

- Propioceptive functioning, which is the capacity to receive stimulation coming from the interior of the organism, achieving better adaptation and "poly-sensory integration", with the domination of the body, notion of the lateral, of space, and of body positioning.

- Psychomotor skills, development of the awareness of the action of the motor and balance coordination.

- The multiple intelligences.

- The "know how", logical-mathematical knowledge, knowing one's own limits and inter-personal relations.

- Self-confidence, giving the individual possibilities of overcoming "oneself", as well as overcoming one's fears.

- The cardio-vascular system, increasing the volume of oxygen, which is carried to all the cells of the body through the blood, diminishing the cardiac frequency of rest and increasing its conditioning as well as making the arteries more flexible by decreasing the adhesion of fat tissue on its walls, reducing the blood pressure by facilitating the return of blood.

- The Muscular-Skeleton System, working the muscles, benefiting stamina, tone and developing of the thoracic muscles, improving the intake of oxygen.

- The Nervous and Psychological System, because it is an activity to free up tensions and diminish stress, regulating the hours of sleep, of rest, and of appetite, strengthening self-confidence, co-existence, socialization, and discipline.

This system allows the one who learns it to dominate an adversary who is physically stronger with a minimum of energy expenditure, utilizing the skill that one acquires with the training of the different exercises and the detailed practice of the Jiu-Jitsu techniques placed in order of progressive movements, without making the use of violence necessary.

The Kioto System does not try to create supermen or super-children, rather its practitioners become people who are psychologically sure of themselves and extremely confident of their skills, facilitating the resolution of extreme situations, even under great physical or psychological pressure, without losing self-control and respect for fellow man.

(Grand Master Francisco Mansur)

The history of Jiu-Jitsu

In the north of India, some 4,500 years ago, the prince Sidhartha Guatama was born, called Saquia Muni (solitary prince), who was later known as Buddha (The Illuminated), giving origin to the religion that took his name, Buddhism.

His followers, monks from faraway monasteries, in order to propagate their faith and engage in commerce to survive, were obliged to make long walks along roads invested with thieves, and due to the impossibility of using weapons for their defense—it being against the morality of their religion—the monks were constant victims of assaults that sometimes cost them their lives. These monks were then forced to create an effective way of resolving the problem. Greatly knowledgeable of the human body and of physical laws like action and reaction, leverage, moment of strength, centrifugal force, inertia, etc., they were without a doubt the true creators of Jiu-Jitsu, the most effective science of fighting in the world, which has defense as its essential principle.

With the death of Buddha, Sidarmamprivia Privadarcen (known as King Asoca) took power, spreading the preaching of Buddhism, and consequently of Jiu-Jitsu, throughout Asia. In this way, going down to Siam, Burma, Thailand, Tibet, and later China, he created in his trajectory innumerable fighting modes based on the science of Jiu-Jitsu, until finally reaching Japan around 2,000 BC, where after separating from religion, it had great impulse, multiplied, and eventually gave rise to the Samurais and Martial Arts.

In feudal Japan, Jiu-Jitsu was comprised of 113 distinct styles, which included the use of the body, hands, arms, legs, feet, and diverse weapons of the epoch, all of that with the use of physical laws, giving rise to this science from which nowadays only 64 styles are known by a few Grand Masters.

In 1886, a North American squad, under the command of the brigadier general White Perry, arrived in Japan and in a friendly way opened the doors of Japan to the world. The North Americans, thirsty for the knowledge of the science of Jiu-Jitsu, which allowed a weak man to overcome a strong man, became a grave problem for the people of the empire of the rising sun, who would lose their hegemony with the big and strong Americans given that they would also know the secrets of Jiu-Jitsu. It then became registered in the Japanese penal code that teaching this science to foreigners was a crime of treason. The secrets of the science of Jiu-Jitsu was taken to the mountains of Kosen. The Master Jigoro Kano was the chosen one. He developed the Jiu-Jitsu techniques of unbalancing and throwing, creating what was at that time called "Jiu-Jitsu" in order to trick the foreigners, later it was called Kano Jiu-Jitsu, and in 1890 it was denominated Judo, with the founding of the Kodokan.

The arrival of Jiu-Jitsu in Brazil was approximately at the beginning of the 20th century, through Mituyo Maeda, Grand Master in Japanese Jiu-Jitsu, known as the Count of Koma—a title he received in Spain for his memorable fights around the world—who, as a representative of his country for the commerce of chestnuts, settled in the city of Belen, the Brazilian state of Para, where he transmitted his knowledge to Carlos Gracie, older brother of the five sons of Gaston Gracie. But, the inspiration came for the Grand Master Helio Gracie, the youngest of the clan, who for not having strength and who was in poor physical condition due to a congenital disease, carried out the transformation of the old Japanese Jiu-Jitsu to what is today practiced around the world with the name of Brazilian Jiu-Jitsu.

Great challenges, memorable fights, "Brazil against the world", all starred the Jiu-Jitsu Grand Master Helio Gracie and his followers from inside and outside the family. Today,

Brazilian Jiu-Jitsu is the most practiced sport after soccer.

Francisco Mansur, black belt and licensed disciple of Grand Master Helio Gracie, inspired by the fact that the contents of the science of Jiu-Jitsu went much further than a simple art of fighting, founded in 1965 a progressive system of movements specifically oriented toward education, the movements of the KIOTO SYSTEM OF BRAZILIAN JIU-JITSU. This system has exclusive exercises with specialized movements.

The KIOTO SYSTEM OF BRAZILIAN JIU-JITSU is comprised of 42 learning levels; each level is comprised of 42 classes prepared progressively and which contain different exercises for adults and children of both sexes, and even for people who need special attention, people with some physical or psychological deficiency.

The Learning Levels are distributed in the following way:

- 15 Levels of 42 classes each level, with kimono, for adults
- 9 Levels of 42 classes each level, with kimono, for children from 4-12 years old
- 6 Levels of 42 classes each level, without use of kimono, for adults
- 3 Levels of 42 classes each level, of Vale-Tudo for adults
- 3 Levels of 30 classes each level, of Self-defense
- 2 Levels of 30 classes each level, of defenses against rape
- 2 Levels of 30 classes each level, of Police Practice
- 2 Levels of 42 classes each level, of submission defenses

The students' belt and grade exams are done twice a year at a pre-established date with the presence of Grand Master Francisco Mansur or of the teacher Krauss Mansor, and they follow the criteria:

4 to 6 years old: White Belt, White with Black Tip, Grey

7 to 9: White Belt, White with Black Tip, Yellow

10-12: White Belt, White with Black Tip, Yellow and Orange

13-15: White Belt, White with Black Tip, Yellow, Orange and Green

16-17: White Belt, White with Black Tip, Blue, Purple and Brown

18 years old and up: White Belt, White with Black Tip, Blue, Purple, Brown, and Black.

The teachers and instructors of the System are authorized by the appropriate organizations that oversee Jiu-Jitsu in Brazil and around the world. There are also leading athletes in national and international competitions with various titles, specialized not only in sportive Jiu-Jitsu for children and adults, but also in the teaching of Self-defense, Police Tactics, and rape defenses.

All the instructors are personally prepared by Grand Master Francisco Mansur or by Krauss Mansor.

The instructors can only give classes conforming to the level in which they were prepared, qualified, and authorized.

It is obligatory for all teachers already trained as black belts of the System to do an annual revision, which is free, for the up-dating of new techniques.

All the belts have 4 grades that go on the black point of the belt.

The black belt has 6 grades, prerogative of the Brazilian Confederation.

In the academic year in which the student is going to turn 16, he or she will be elevated to the adult belt corresponding to the belt that he has at the time of the change of age.

Grand Master Francisco Mansur, 9th Degree Red Belt from the Brazilian Confederation and the International

Brazilian Jiu-Jitsu Federation, is the technical and intellectual author of KIOTO SYSTEM OF BRAZILIAN JIU-JITSU, being the sole owner of the intellectual rights and as founder of the system.

FUNDAMENTOS
FOUNDATIONS
FUNDAMENTOS
GRUNDLAGEN
FONDEMENTS
FONDAMENTI

Posições de Base em Pé, Ajoelhado e Agachado

Basic Standing, Kneeling, and Squatting positions

Posiciones de Base de Pie, Arrodillado y Agachado

Grundstellungen im Stand, kniend und gebeugt

Positions de Base debout, a genoux et incliné

Posizione in Piedi Basilare, Inginocchiato e Chinato

• **1ª Base em pé. Lateral** • 1st Standing base. Lateral • **1ª Base de pie. Lateral** • **1. Seitlicher Stand** • **1ᵉʳ Base debout. Latérale** • **1ª Base in piedi. Laterale**

• **2ª Base em pé. Ataque** • 2nd Standing base. Attack • **2ª Base de pie. Ataque** • **2. Angriff** • **2ᵉ Base debout. Attaque** • **2ª Base in piedi. Attacco**

• **3ª Base em pé. Defesa** • 3rd Standing base. Defense • **3ª Base de pie. Defensa** • **3. Verteidigung** • **3ᵉ Base debout. Défénse** • **Base in piedi. Difesa**

- **4ª Base em pé. Ataque nas pernas**
- 4th Standing base. Attack to the legs
- **4ª Base de pie. Ataque a las piernas**
- **4. Angriff zu den Beinen**
- **4º Base debout. Attaque aux jambes**
- **4ª Base in piedi. Attacco alle gambe**

- **5ª Base em pé. Sumo base frontal**
- 5th Standing base. Frontal sumo base
- **5ª Base de pie. Sumo base frontal**
- **5. Frontal, Sumo**
- **5º Base debout. Sumo base frontale**
- **5ª Base in piedi. Sumo base frontale**

- **5ª Base em pé. Sumo base lateral** • 5th Standing base. Side sumo base
- **5ª Base de pie. Sumo base lateral** • **5. Sumo seitlich** • **5º Base debout. Sumo base latérale** • **5ª Base in piedi. Sumo base laterale**

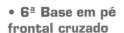

- **6ª Base em pé frontal cruzado**
- 6th Frontal standing base crossed
- **6ª Base de pie frontal cruzado**
- **6. Frontal**
- **6º Base debout frontale**
- **6ª Base in piedi frontale**

- **1ª Base agachado**
- 1st Squatting base
- **1ª Base de pie agachado**
- **1. Grundstellung gebeugt**
- **1er Base debout incliné**
- **1ª Base in piedi chinato**

- **2ª Base agachado**
- 2st Squatting base
- **2ª Base de pie agachado**
- **2. Grundstellung gebeugt**
- **2e Base debout. Latérale**
- **2ª Base in piedi chinato**

- **3ª Base agachado**
- 3st Squatting base
- **3ª Base de pie agachado**
- **3. Grundstellung gebeugt**
- **3e Base debout incliné**
- **3ª Base in piedi chinato**

- 1ª Base ajoelhado
- 1st Kneeling base
- 1ª Base arrodillado
- 1. Grundstellung kniend
- 1er Base à genoux
- 1ª Base inginocchiato

- 4ª Base ajoelhado. O andar do Samurai
- 4th Kneeling base. The Samurai Walk
- 4ª Base arrodillado. El caminar del Samurai
- 4. Grundstellung kniend. Der Gang des Samurai
- 4º Base à genoux. Marche du Samouraï
- 4ª Base inginocchiato. Il camminare del Samurai

- 2ª Base ajoelhado
- 2nd Kneeling base
- 2ª Base arrodillado
- 2. Grundstellung kniend
- 2ᵉ Base à genoux
- 2ª Base inginocchiato

- 3ª Base ajoelhado
- 3rd Kneeling base
- 3ª Base arrodillado
- 3. Grundstellung kniend
- 3ᵉ Base à genoux
- 3ª Base inginocchiato

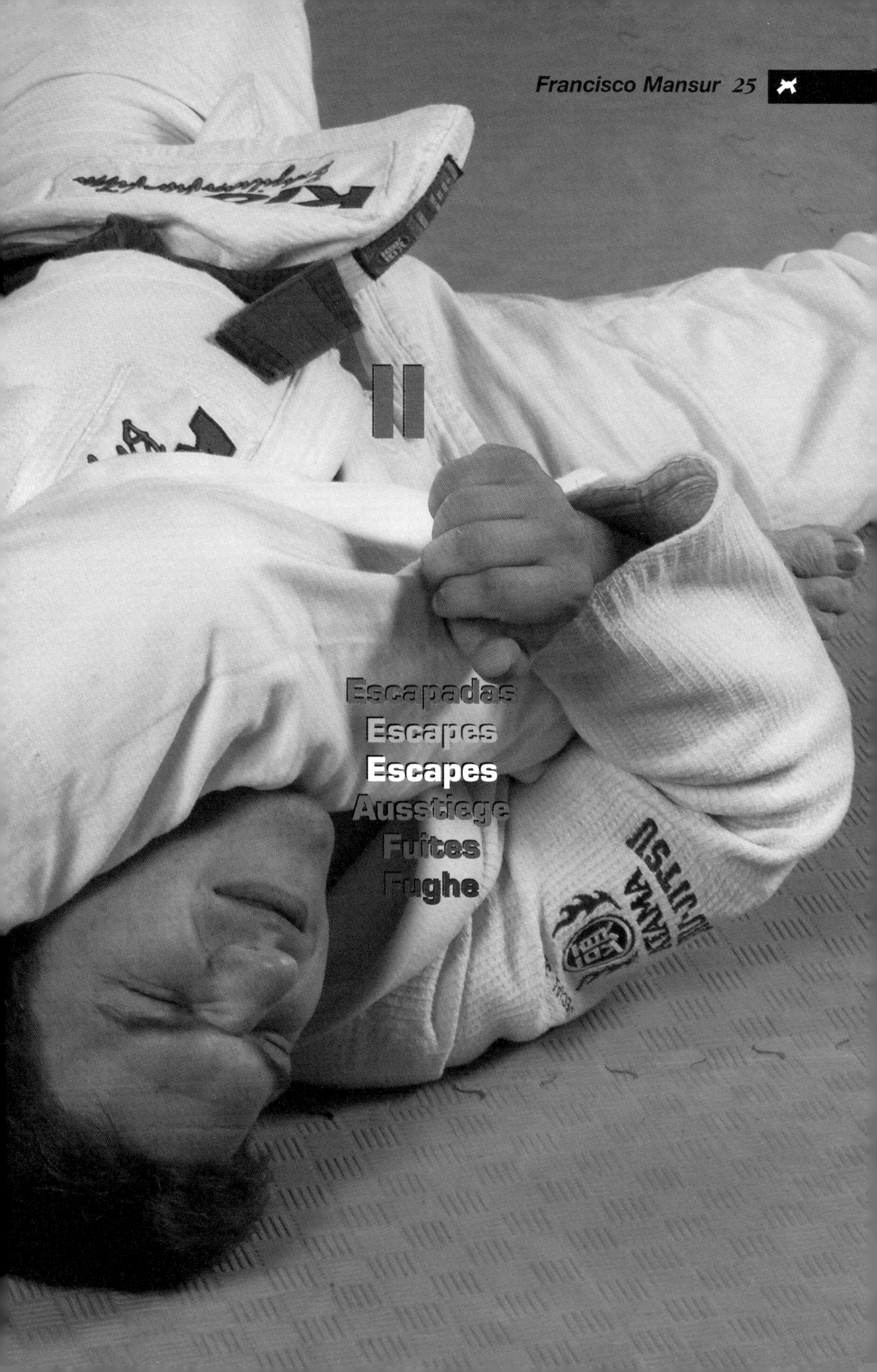

II

Escapadas
Escapes
Escapes
Ausstiege
Fuites
Fughe

- **1ª Escapada de quadril** • 1st Hip escape • **1º Escape de caderas**
- **1. Hüftausstieg** • **1ᵉʳ Fuites de hanches** • **1º Fuga di fianchi**

- **2ª Escapada de ombro** • 2nd Shoulder escape • **2º Escape de hombro**
- **2. Schulterausstieg** • **2ᵉ Fuites d'épaule** • **2º Fuga di spalla**

- 3ª Escapada inversa • 3rd Inverse escape • 3º Escape inverso
- 3. Invertierter Ausstieg • 3e Fuite inverse • 3º Fuga inversa

• 4ª Escapada quadril em círculo • 4th Circular hip escape • 4º Escape caderas en círculo • 4. Kreisender Hüftausstieg • 4º Fuite de hanches en rond • 4º Fuga fianchi circolare

- 5ª Ombro em círculo • 5th Circular shoulder escape • 5º Hombro en circulo
- 5. Kreisende Schulter • 5º Epaule en rond • 5º Spalla circolare

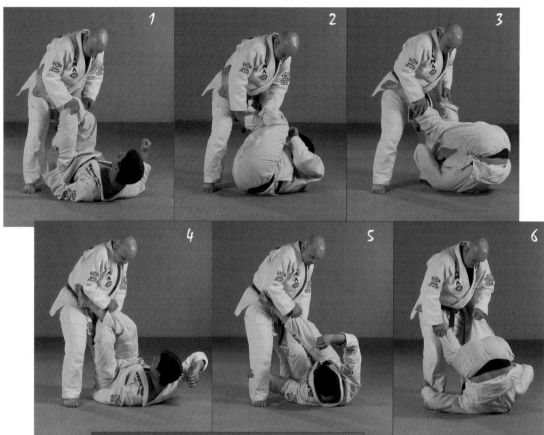

- 6ª Pião
- 6th Spinning
- 6º Peonza
- 6. Kreisel
- 6º Toupie
- 6º Trottola

- **7ª Escapada "side wonder"**
- 7th "Side wonder" escape
- **7º Escape "side wonder"**
- **7. Ausstieg „side wonder"**
- **7º Fuite "side wonder"**
- **7ª Fuga "side wonder"**

- **8ª Escapada "Break Dance"** • 8th "Break dance" escape • **8ª Escape "Break Dance"** • **8. Ausstieg „Break Dance"** • **8º Fuite "Break Dance"** • **8ª Fuga "Break Dance"**

- 9ª Escapada. Ataque da aranha • 9th "Spider attack" escape
- 9º Escape "Ataque de la araña" • 9. Ausstieg „Angriff der Spinne"
- 9º Fuite "Attaque de l'araignée" • 9º Fuga "Attacco del ragno"

- 10ª Escapada. Levantada técnica
- 10th Lifting escape technique
- 10º Escape levantada técnica
- 10. Ausstieg, erhöhte Technik
- 10º Fuite technique levée
- 10º Fuga alzata tecnica

• **11ª Escapada. Norte - Sul (giro polar)** • 11th North-South (polar turn)
• **11ª Norte - Sur (giro polar)** • **11. Nord-Süd** • **11er Nord - Sud (cercle polaire)** • **11ª Nord - Sud (giro polare)**

• **"Ponte"** • "Bridge" • **"Puente"** • **„Brücke"** • **Pont** • **"Ponte"**

III

Caidas • Ukemi
Takedown • Ukemi
Caidas • Ukemi
Fallschule • Ukemi
Chutes • Ukemi
Cadute • Ukemi

- **Caidas de costas**
  - Back Takedown
- **Caídas de espalda**
  - **Fallen auf den Rücken**
  - **Chutes d'épaule**
- **Cadute di schiena**

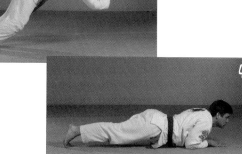

- Caidas de frente
- Front takedown
- Caídas de frente
- Fallen nach vorn
- Chutes de face
- Cadute in avanti

- **Caídas de lado** • Side takedown • **Caídas de lado** • **Fallen auf die Seite**
- **Chutes de côté** • **Cadute di lato**

- **Rolamento**
- Turned
- **Rodada**
- **Rolle**
- **Roulée**
- **Ruotata**

TECNICAS
TECHNIQUES
TECNICAS
TECHNIKEN
TECHNIQUES
TECNICHE

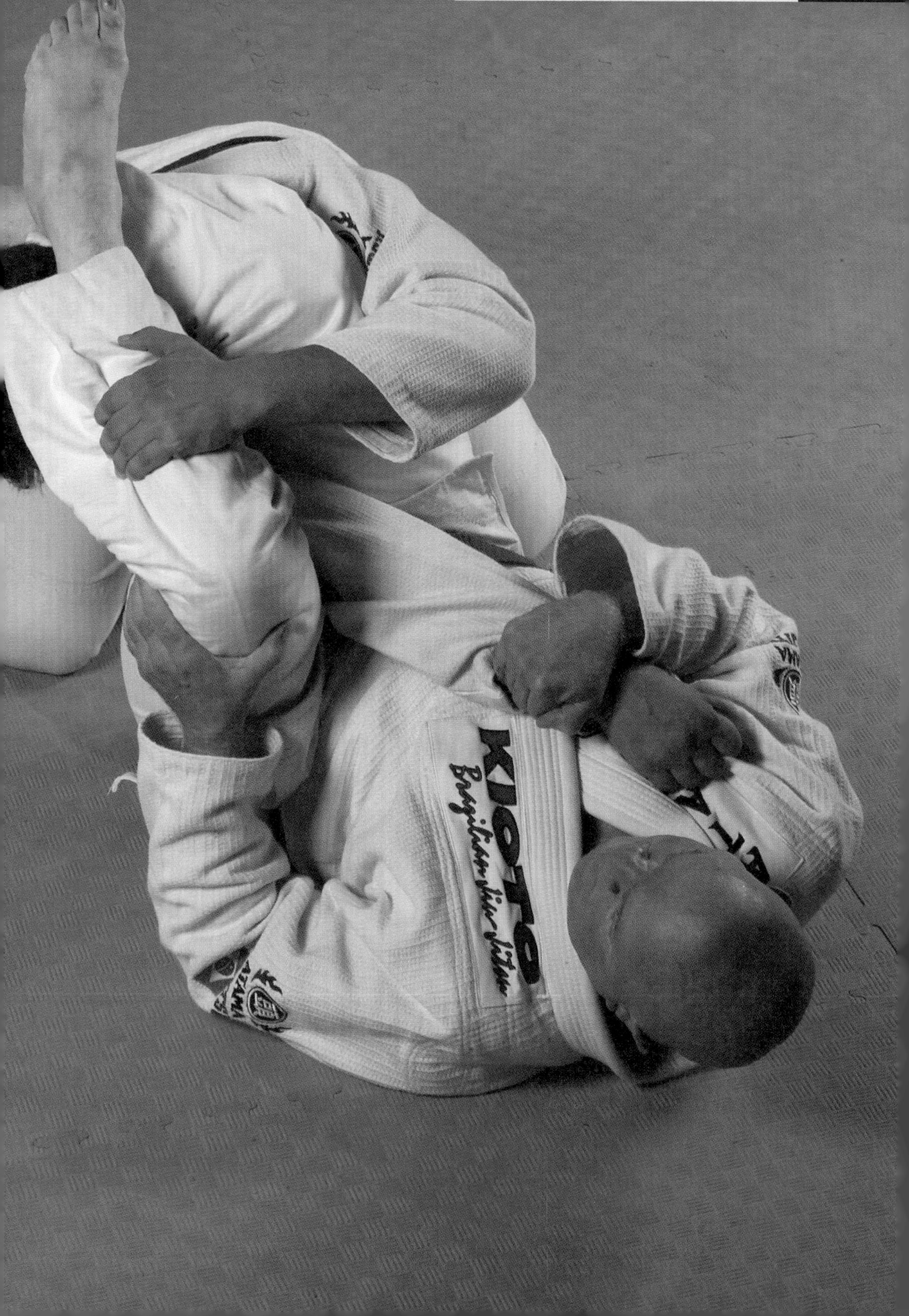
KIOTO

IV

"Montadas" Posições e Defesa
"Mounted" positions and defense
"Montadas" Posiciones y Defensa
„Montadas" (Reiterstellungen)
Positionen und Verteidigung
"Montées" Positions et Défenses
"Montada" Posizioni e Difesa

- **1ª Posição Montado**
- 1st Mounted position
- **1ª Posición Montado**
- **1. Reiterstellung**
- **1er Position Monté**
- **1ª Posizione Montada**

- **2ª Posição Montado**
- 2nd Mounted position
- **2ª Posición Montado**
- **2. Reiterstellung**
- **2e Position Monté**
- **2ª Posizione Montada**

- **3ª Posição Montado**
- 3rd Mounted position
- **3ª Posición Montado**
- **3. Reiterstellung**
- **3e Position Monté**
- **3ª Posizione Montada**

- **4ª Posição Montado**
- 4th Mounted position
- **4ª Posición Montado**
- **4. Reiterstellung**
- **4e Position Monté**
- **4ª Posizione Montada**

- **1ª Defesa da montada**
- 1st Mounted defense
- **1ª Defensa de la montada**
- **1. Verteidigung der Reiterstellung**
- **1er Défense de la montée**
- **1ª Difesa dalla montada**

• **2ª Defesa da montada** • 2nd Mounted defense • **2ª Defensa de la montada** • **2. Verteidigung der Reiterstellung** • **2ᵉ Défense de la montée** • **2ª Difesa dalla montada**

- 3ª **Defesa da montada**
- 3rd **Mounted defense**
- 3ª **Defensa de la montada**
- 3. **Verteidigung der Reiterstellung**
- 3e **Défense de la montée**
- 3ª **Difesa dalla montada**

- **4ª Defesa da montada**
- 4th Mounted defense
- **4ª Defensa de la montada**
- **4. Verteidigung der Reiterstellung**
- **4ᵉ Défense de la montée**
- **4ª Difesa dalla montada**

V

Posições de guarda. Puxada para a Guarda. Passagens de guarda. Ajoelhado e em pe
Guard positions. Pull toward the guard. Guard passes. Kneeling and standing
Posiciones de guardia. Tirón hacia la Guardia. Pasadas de guardia. Arrodillado y de pie
Positionen der Deckung.
Angriff auf die Deckung. Durchdringen der Deckung. Kniend und im Stand
Positions de garde. Tirer vers la Garde. Passages de garde. A genoux et debout
Posizioni di guardia. Tirare verso la Guardia. Passaggi di guardia. Inginocchiato ed in piedi

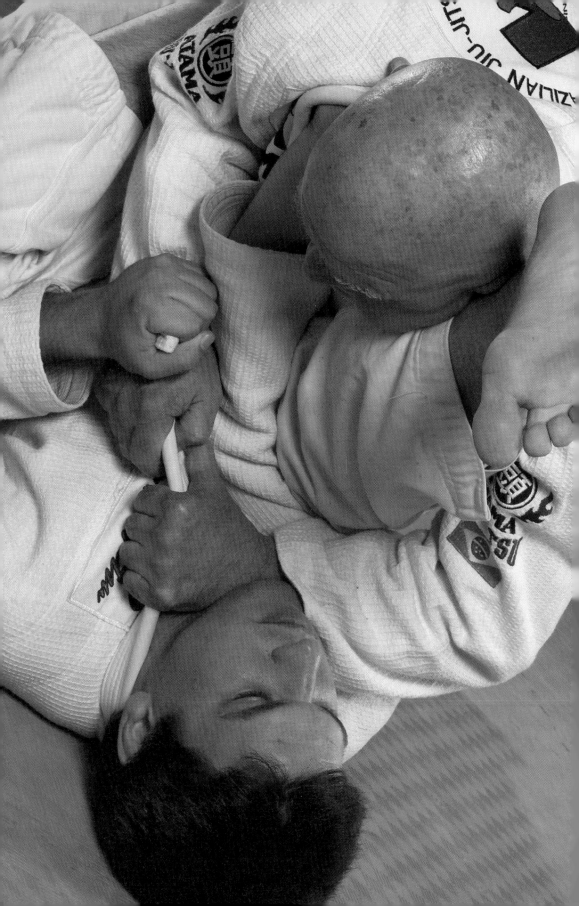

• 1ª Posição de guarda no ataque ajoelhado • 1st guard position in kneeling attack • 1ª Posición de guardia en el ataque arrodillado • 1. Deckungsposition im knienden Angriff • 1er Position de garde dans l'attaque à genoux • 1ª Posizione di guardia nell'attacco inginocchiato

• 2ª Posição de guarda no ataque ajoelhado • 2nd guard position in kneeling attack • 2ª Posición de guardia en el ataque arrodillado 2. Deckungsposition im knienden Angriff • 2e Position de garde dans l'attaque à genoux • 2ª Posizione di guardia nell'attacco inginocchiato

• 3ª Posição de guarda no ataque ajoelhado • 3rd guard position in kneeling attack • 3ª Posición de guardia en el ataque arrodillado • 3. Deckungsposition im knienden Angriff • 3e Position de garde dans l'attaque à genoux • 3ª Posizione di guardia nell'attacco inginocchiato

• 4ª Posição de guarda no ataque ajoelhado • 4th guard position in kneeling attack • 4ª Posición de guardia en el ataque arrodillado 4. Deckungsposition im knienden Angriff • 4e Position de garde dans l'attaque à genoux • 4ª Posizione di guardia nell'attacco inginocchiato

- **1ª Posição de guarda no ataque em pé** • 1st Guard position in standing attack • **1ª Posición de guardia en el ataque de pie** • **1. Deckungsposition im stehenden Angriff** • **1ᵉʳ Position de garde dans l'attaque debout**
- **1ª Posizione di guardia nell'attacco in piedi**

- **2ª Posição de guarda no ataque em pé** • 2nd Guard position in standing attack • **2ªPposición de guardia en el ataque de pie** • **2. Deckungsposition im stehenden Angriff** • **2ᵉ Position de garde dans l'attaque debout**
- **1ª Posizione di guardia nell'attacco in piedi**

• **3ª Posição de guarda no ataque em pé** • 3rd Guard position in standing attack
• **3ª Posición de guardia en el ataque de pie** • **3. Deckungsposition im stehenden Angriff** • **3ᵉ Position de garde dans l'attaque debout**
• **3ª Posizione di guardia nell'attacco in piedi**

• **4ª Posição de guarda no ataque em pé** • 4thGguard position in standing attack
• **4ª Posición de guardia en el ataque de pie**
• **4. Deckungsposition im stehenden Angriff**
• **4ᵉ Position de garde dans l'attaque debout**
• **4ª Posizione di guardia nell'attacco in piedi**

- **Puxada para a guarda** • Pull toward the guard • **Trón hacia la guardia**
- **Angriff auf die Deckung** • **Tirer vers la garde** • **Tirare verso la guardia**

- **1ª Pasagem de guarda ajoelhado** • 1st Passing the guard kneeling
- **1ª Pasar de guardia arrodillado** • **1. Durchdringen der Deckung, kniend**
- **1er Passage de garde à genoux** • **1° Passaggio di guardia inginocchiato**

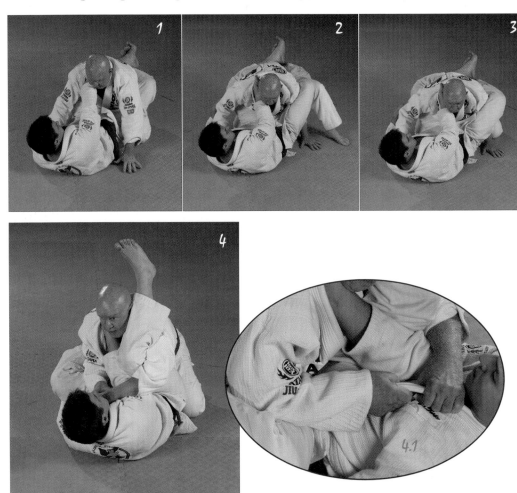

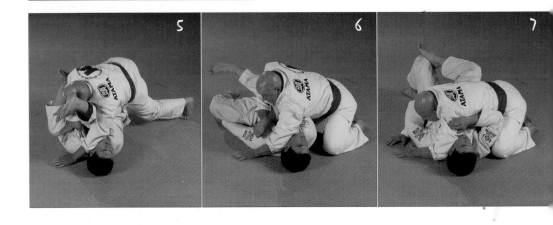

- **2ª Pasagem de guarda ajoelhado**
- 2nd Passing the guard kneeling
- **2ª Pasar de guardia arrodillado**
- **2. Durchdringen der Deckung, kniend**
- **2ᵉ Passage de garde à genoux**
- **2° Passaggio di guardia inginocchiato**

- 3ª **Pasagem de guarda ajoelhado**
- 3rd Passing the guard kneeling
- 3ª **Pasar de guardia arrodillado**
- 3. **Durchdringen der Deckung, kniend**
- 3e **Passage de garde à genoux**
- 3° **Passaggio di guardia inginocchiato**

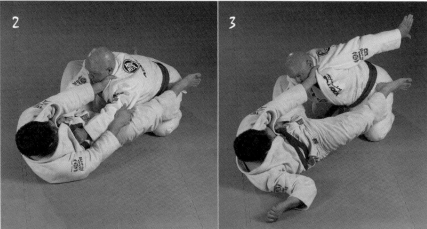

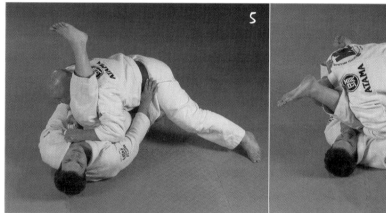

- **4ª Pasagem de guarda ajoelhado**
- **4th Passing the guard kneeling**
- **4ª Pasar de guardia arrodillado**
- **4. Durchdringen der Deckung, kniend**
- **4e Passage de garde à genoux**
- **4° Passaggio di guardia inginocchiato**

- **1ª Passagem de guarda em pé** • **1st Passing the guard standing**
- **1ª Pasada de guardia de pie** • **1. Durchdringen der Deckung, stehend**
- **1er Passage de garde debout** • **1° Passaggio di guardia in piedi**

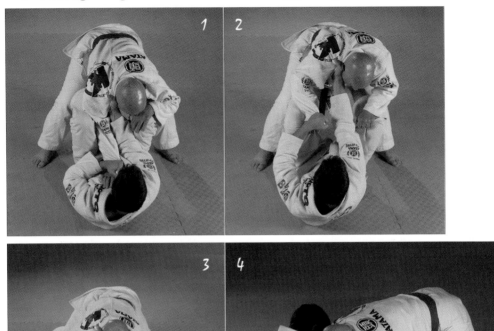

- **2ª Passagem de guarda em pé** • 2nd Passing the guard standing
- **2ª Base de pie. Lateral** • **2. Durchdringen der Deckung, stehend**
- **2ᵉ Passage de garde debout** • **2° Passaggio di guardia in piedi**

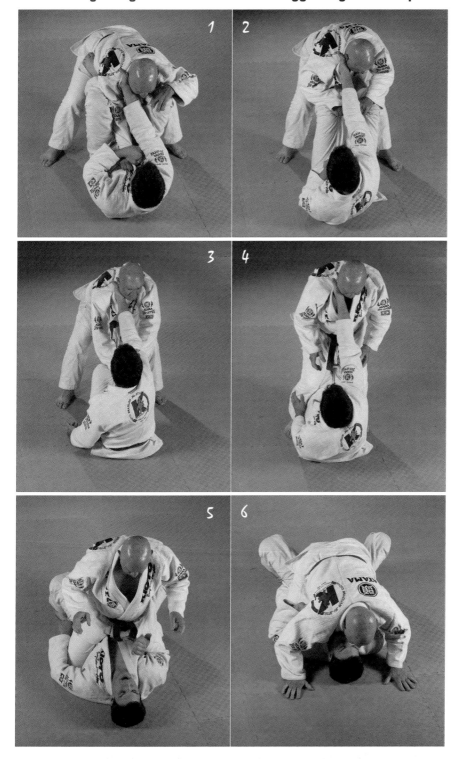

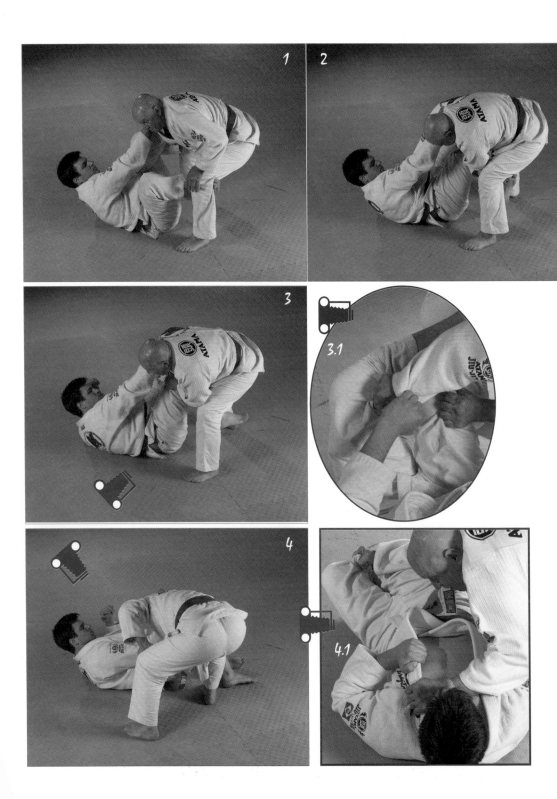

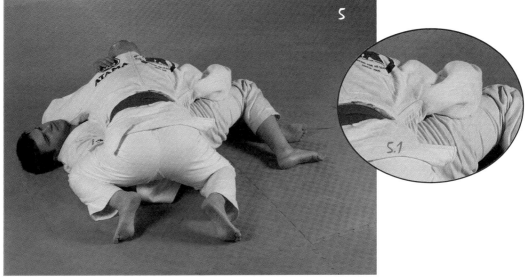

- **3ª Passagem de guarda em pé**
- 3rd Passing the guard standing
- **3er Pasar de guardia de pie**
- **3. Durchdringen der Deckung, stehend**
- **3e Passage de garde debout**
- **3° Passaggio di guardia in piedi**

- **4ª Passagem de guarda em pé**
- **4th Passing the guard standing**
- **4ª Pasada de guardia de pie**
- **4. Durchdringen der Deckung, stehend**
- **4ᵉ Passage de garde debout**
- **4° Passaggio di guardia in piedi**

- **5ª Passagem de guarda em pé** • 5th Passing the guard standing
- **5ª Pasada de guardia de pie** • **5. Durchdringen der Deckung, stehend**
- **5ᵉ Passage de garde debout** • **5° Passaggio di guardia in piedi**

VI

Raspagens Ajoelhado e em Pe
Kneeling and standing scrapes
Raspados Arrodillado y de Pie
Raspado, im Stand und kniend
Raspados à genoux et debout
Raspado Inginocchiato ed in piedi

• **1ª Raspagem ajoelhado** • 1st Kneeling scrape • **1º Raspado arrodillado** • **1. Raspado, kniend** • **1ᵉʳ "Raspado" (renversement) à genoux** • **1º Raspado inginocchiato**

• **2ª Raspagem ajoelhado** • 2nd Kneeling scrape • **2º Raspado arrodillado**
• **2. Raspado, kniend** • **2ᵉ Raspado à genoux**
• **2ª 2º Raspado inginocchiato**

• **3ª Raspagem ajoelhado** • 3rd Kneeling scrape • **3º Raspado arrodillado**
• **3. Raspado, kniend** • **3ᵉ Raspado à genoux** • **3º Raspado inginocchiato**

- **4ª Raspagem ajoelhado**
- **4th Kneeling scrape**
- **4º Raspado arrodillado**
- **4. Raspado, kniend**
- **4e Raspado à genoux**
- **4º Raspado inginocchiato**

- **1ª Raspagem em pé.**
- 1st Standing scrape
- **1º Raspado de pie**
- **1. Raspado im Stand**
- **1ᵉʳ Raspado debout**
- **1° Raspado in piedi**

- **2ª Raspagem em pé** • 2nd Standing scrape • **2º Raspado de pie**
- **2. Raspado im Stand** • **2ᵉ Raspado debout** • **2° Raspado in piedi**

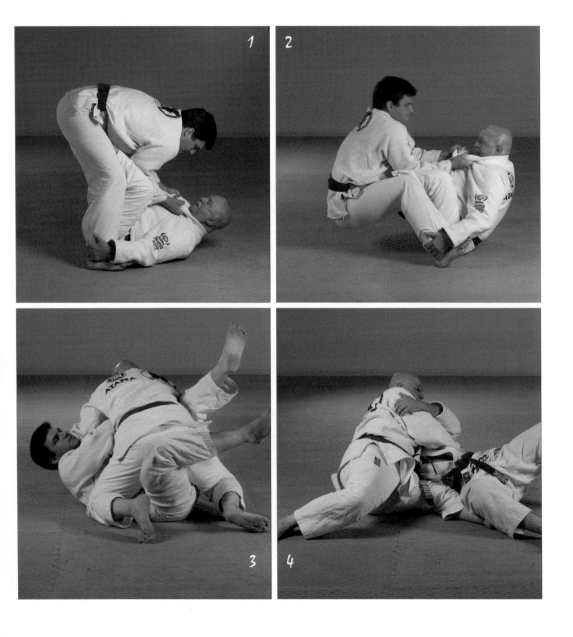

- **3ª Raspagem em pé** • 3rd Standing scrape • **3º Raspado de pie**
- **3. Raspado im Stand** • **3e Raspado debout** • **3° Raspado in piedi**

VII

Imobilizações
Immobilizations
Inmovilizaciones
Immobilisierungen
Immobilisations
Immobilizzazioni

- 1ª Imobilização • 1st Immobilization
- 1ª Inmovilización • 1. Immobilisierung
- 1er Immobilisation • 1ª Immobilizzazione

• **2ª Imobilização** • 2nd Immobilization • **2ª Inmovilización**
• **2. Immobilisierung** • **2ᵉ Immobilisation** • **2ª Immobilizzazione**

- **3ª Imobilização** • 3rd Immobilization • **3ª Inmovilización**
- **3. Immobilisierung** • **3ᵉ Immobilisation** • **3ª Immobilizzazione**

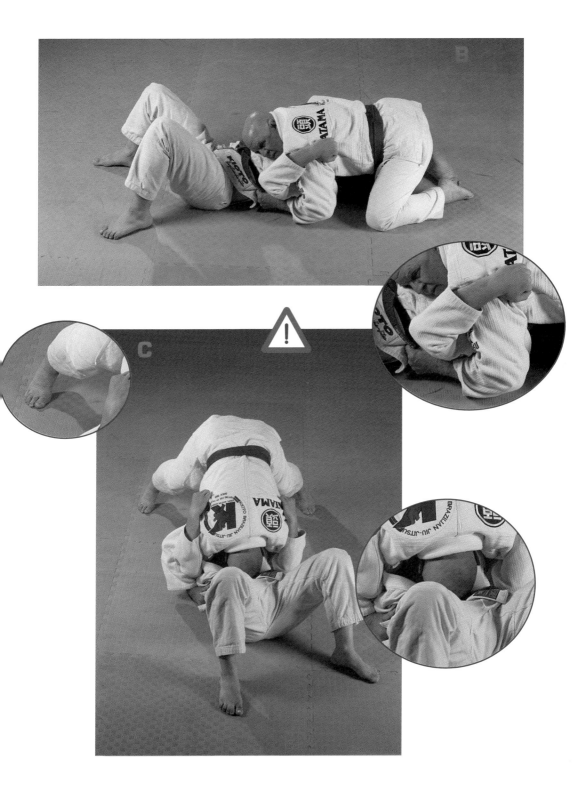

- **4ª Imobilização** • 4th Immobilization • **4ª Inmovilización**
- **4. Immobilisierung** • **4ᵉ Immobilisation** • **4ª Immobilizzazione**

- **5ª Imobilização** • 5th Immobilization • **5ª Inmovilización**
- **5. Immobilisierung** • **5ᵉ Immobilisation** • **5ª Immobilizzazione**

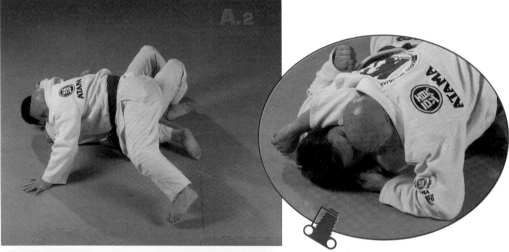

VIII

Estrangulamentos
Chokes
Estrangulaciones
Würgetechniken
Etranglements
Strangolamenti

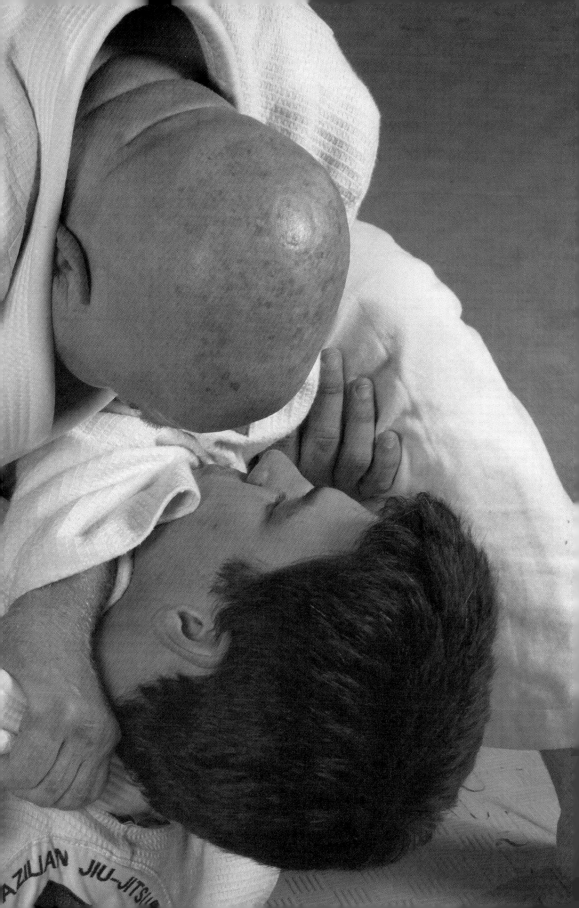

- **1º Estrangulamento em pe** • 1st Standing choke • **1º Estrangulación de pie** • **1. Würgetechnik im Stand** • **1ᵉʳ Etranglement debout**
- **1º Strangolamento in piedi**

- **1º Estrangulamento em guarda** • 1st Choke in guard
- **1ª Estrangulación en guardia** • **1. Würgetechnik in der Deckung**
- **1er Etranglement en garde** • **1ª Strangolamento in guardia**

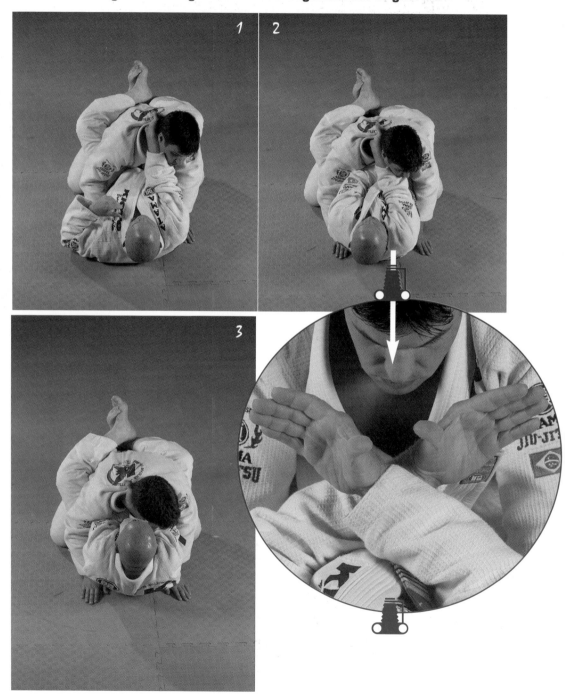

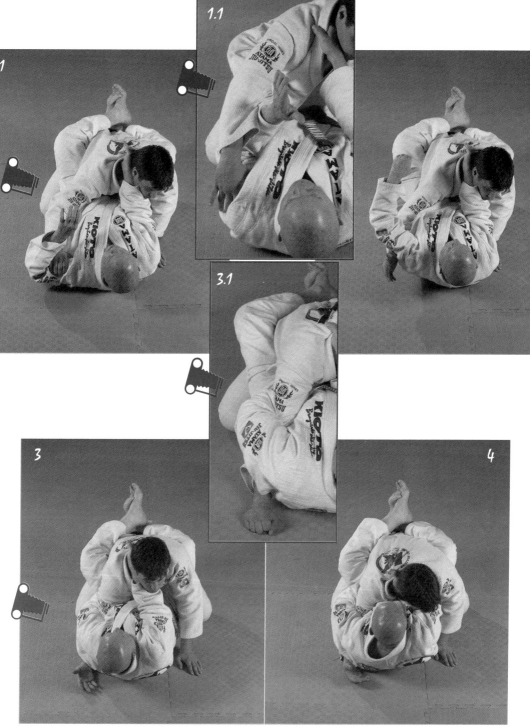

- 2º **Estrangulamento em guarda** • 2nd Choke in guard
- 2ª **Estrangulación en guardia** • 2. **Würgetechnik in der Deckung**
- 2e **Etranglement en garde** • 2ª **Strangolamento in guardia**

- 3º Estrangulamento em guarda • 3rd Choke in guard • 3ª Estrangulación en guardia • 3. Würgetechnik in der Deckung • 3ᵉ Etranglement en garde • 3ª Strangolamento in guardia

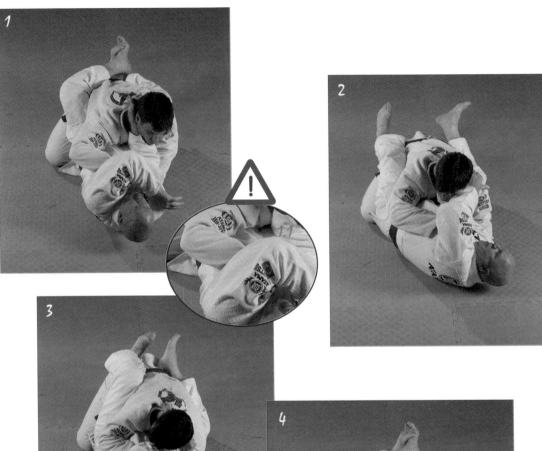

• **4º Estrangulamento em guarda** • 4th Choke in guard • **4ª Estrangulación en guardia** • **4. Würgetechnik in der Deckung** • **4ᵉ Etranglement en garde** • **4ª Strangolamento in guardia**

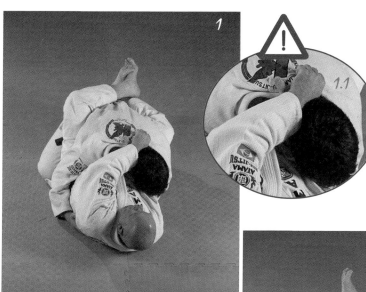

• 5º Estrangulamento em guarda • 5th Choke in guard • 5ª Estrangulación en guardia • 5. Würgetechnik in der Deckung • 5ᵉ Etranglement en garde • 5º Strangolamento in guardia

• **1º Estrangulamento montado** • 1st Mounted choke • **1ª Estrangulación montado** • **1. Würgetechnik in Reiterstellung** • **1ᵉʳ Etranglement monté** • **1° Strangolamento in montada**

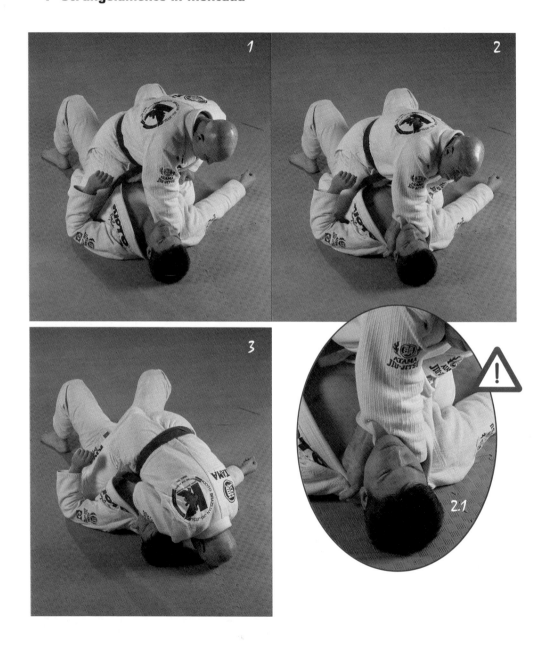

• **2º Estrangulamento montado** • 2nd Mounted choke • **2ª Estrangulación montado** • **2. Würgetechnik in Reiterstellung** • **2ᵉ Etranglement monté**
• **2° Strangolamento in montada**

• **3º Estrangulamento montado** • 3rd Mounted choke • **3ª Estrangulación montado** • **3. Würgetechnik in Reiterstellung** • **3ᵉ Etranglación monté**
• **3° Strangolamento in montada**

- **4º Estrangulamento montado**
- **4th Mounted choke**
- **4ª Estrangulación montado**
- **4. Würgetechnik in Reiterstellung**
- **4ᵉ Etranglement monté**
- **4° Strangolamento in montada**

• **1º Estrangulamento na 1ª imobilização** • 1st Choke in the 1st immobilization • **1ª Estrangulación en la 1ª inmovilización**
• **1. Würgetechnik mit 1. Immobilisierung** • **1ᵉʳ Etranglement dans la 1ᵉʳ immobilisation** • **1ª Strangolamento nella 1ª immobilizzazione**

• **2º Estrangulamento na 1ª imobilização** • 2nd Choke in the 1st immobilization • **2ª Estrangulación en la 1ª inmovilización** • **2. Würgetechnik mit 1. Immobilisierung** • **2ᵉ Etranglement dans la 1ᵉʳ immobilisation**
• **2° Strangolamento nella 1ª immobilizzazione**

- 3º **Estrangulamento na 1ª imobilização**
- 3rd Choke in the 1st immobilization
- 3ª **Estrangulación en la 1ª inmovilización**
- 3. **Würgetechnik mit 1. Immobilisierung**
- 3e **Etranglement dans la 1er immobilisation**
- 3° **Strangolamento nella 1ª immobilizzazione**

- **1º Estrangulamento na 2ª imobilização**
  - 1st Choke in the 2nd immobilization
- **1ª Estrangulación en la 2ª inmovilización**
- **1. Würgetechnik mit 2. Immobilisierung**
- **1er Etranglement dans la 2e immobilisation**
- **1° Strangolamento nella 2ª immobilizzazione**

• **1º Estrangulamento na posição de 4 apoios** • 1st Choke in the 4-support position • **1ª Estrangulación en la posición de 4 apoyos** • **1. Würgetechnik in der Position der vier Stützen** • **1ᵉʳ Etranglement dans la position de 4 appuis** • **1° Strangolamento nella posizione dei 4 appoggi**

• **2º Estrangulamento na posição de 4 apoios** • 2nd ©hoke in the 4-support position • **2ª Estrangulación en la posición de 4 apoyos**
• **2. Würgetechnik in der Position der vier Stützen** • **2ᵉ Etranglement dans la position de 4 appuis** • **2° Strangolamento nella posizione dei 4 appoggi**

• **1º e 2º Estrangulamentos pelas costas** • 1st and 2nd Choke from the back • **1ª y 2ª Estrangulaciones por la espalda** • **1. und 2. Würgetechnik im Rücken** • **1ᵉʳ et 2ᵉ Etranglements par derrière** • **1° e 2° Strangolamenti alle spalle**

• **3º e 4º Estrangulamentos pelas costas** • 3rd and 4th Choke from the back • **3ª y 4ª Estrangulaciones por la espalda** • **3. und 4. Würgetechnik im Rücken** • **3ᵉ et 4ᵉ Etranglements par derrière** • **3° e 4° Strangolamenti alle spalle**

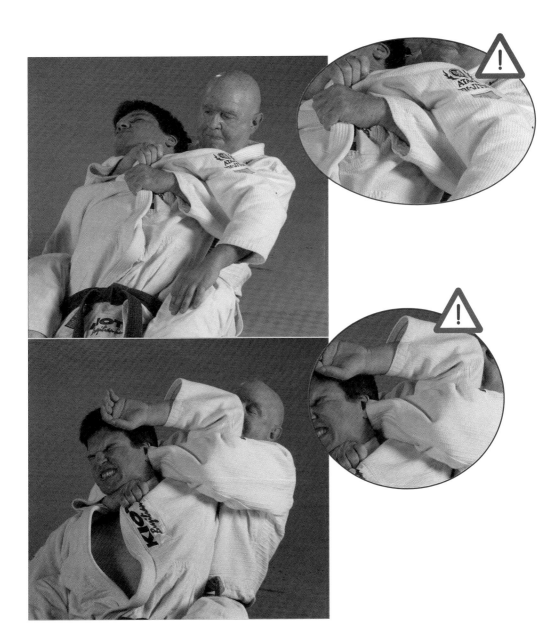

IX

Chave de braço
Arm-lock
Llave de brazo
Armhebel
Clé de bras
Chiave al braccio

• **1ª Chave de braço montado** • 1st Mounted arm-lock • **1ª Llave de brazo montado** • **1. Armhebel, sitzend** • **1ᵉʳ Clé de bras "monté"** • **1ª Chiave al braccio montada**

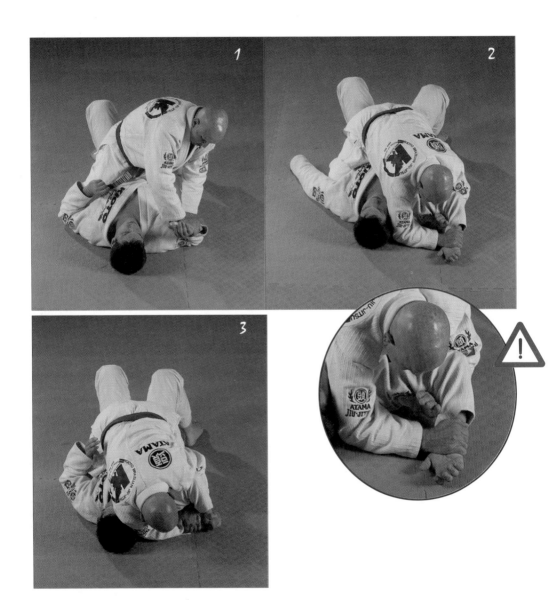

• **1ª Chave de braço na 1ª imobilização** • 1st Arm-lock in the 1st immobilization • **1ª Llave de brazo en la 1ª inmovilización • 1. Armhebel, sitzend • 1ᵉʳ Clé de bras dans la 1ᵉʳ immobilisation • 1ª Chiave al braccio nella 1ª immobilizzazione**

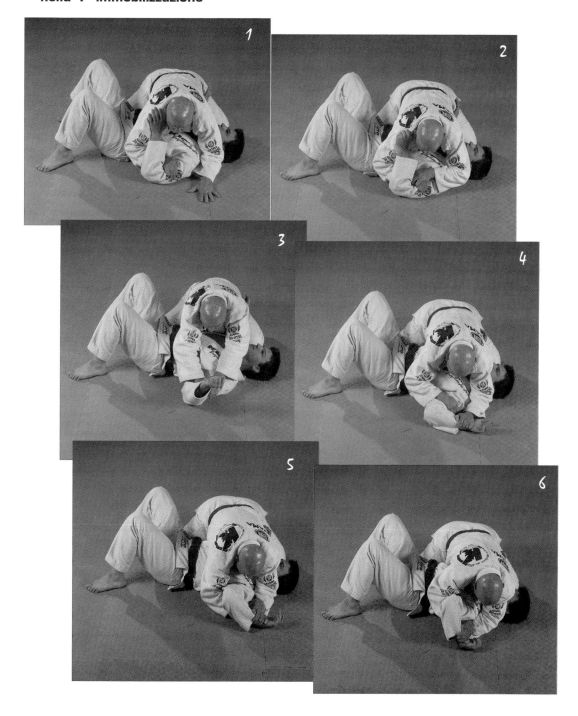

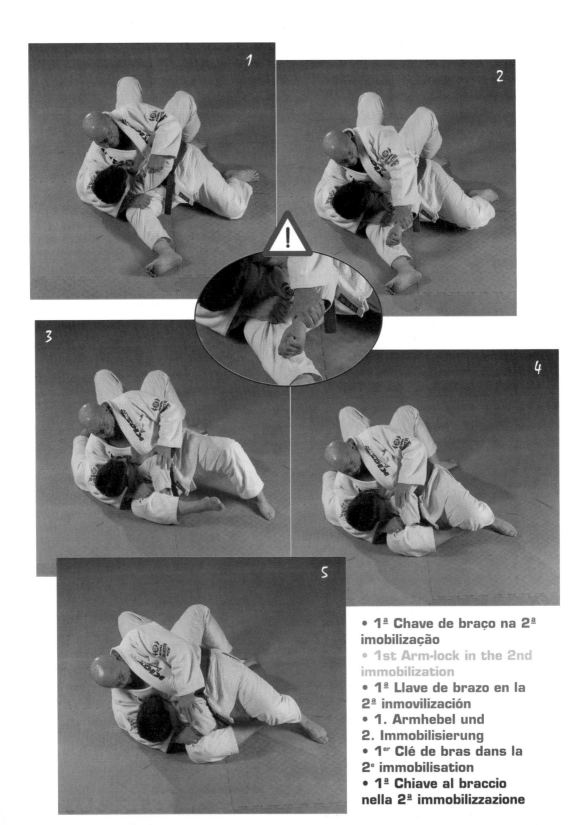

- 1ª Chave de braço na 2ª imobilização
- 1st Arm-lock in the 2nd immobilization
- 1ª Llave de brazo en la 2ª inmovilización
- 1. Armhebel und 2. Immobilisierung
- 1er Clé de bras dans la 2e immobilisation
- 1ª Chiave al braccio nella 2ª immobilizzazione

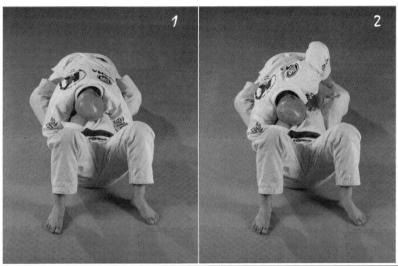

- **1ª Chave de braço na 3ª imobilização**
- 1st Arm-lock in the 3rd immobilization
- **1ª Llave de brazo en la 3ª inmovilización**
- **1. Armhebel und 3. Immobilisierung**
- **1er Clé de bras dans la 3e immobilisation**
- **1ª Chiave al braccio nella 3ª immobilizzazione**

• **1ª Chave de braço em Guarda** • 1st Arm-lock in guard • **1ª Llave de brazo en Guardia** • **1. Armhebel in Deckung** • **1ᵉʳ Clé de bras en Garde** • **1ª Chiave al braccio in Guardia**

X

Posições em pé na guarda
Standing guard positions
Posiciones de pie en la guardia
Fußpositionen in der Deckung
Positions debout dans la garde
Posizioni in piedi nella guardia

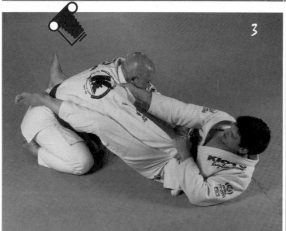

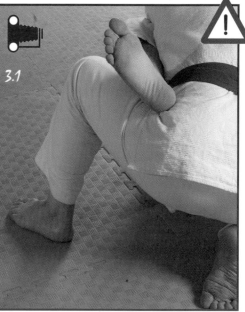

- 1ª Posição em pé na guarda
- 1st Standing guard position
- 1ª Posición de pie en la guardia
- 1. Fußposition in der Deckung
- 1er Position debout dans la garde
- 1ª Posizione in piedi nella guardia

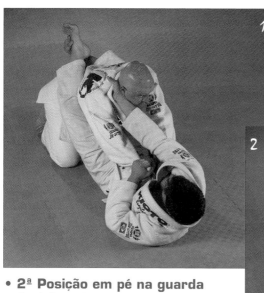

- **2ª Posição em pé na guarda**
- 2nd Standing guard position
- **2ª Posición de pie en la guardia**
- **2. Fußposition in der Deckung**
- **2ᵉ Position debout dans la garde**
- **2ª Posizione in piedi nella guardia**

• **3ª Posição em pé na guarda** • 3rd Standing guard position • **3ª Posición de pie en la guardia** • **3. Fußposition in der Deckung** • **3ᵉ Position debout dans la garde** • **3ª Posizione in piedi nella guardia**

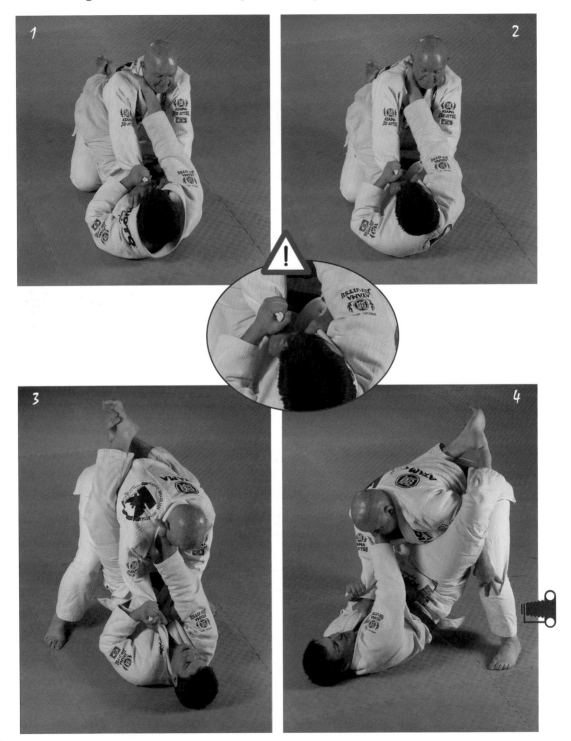

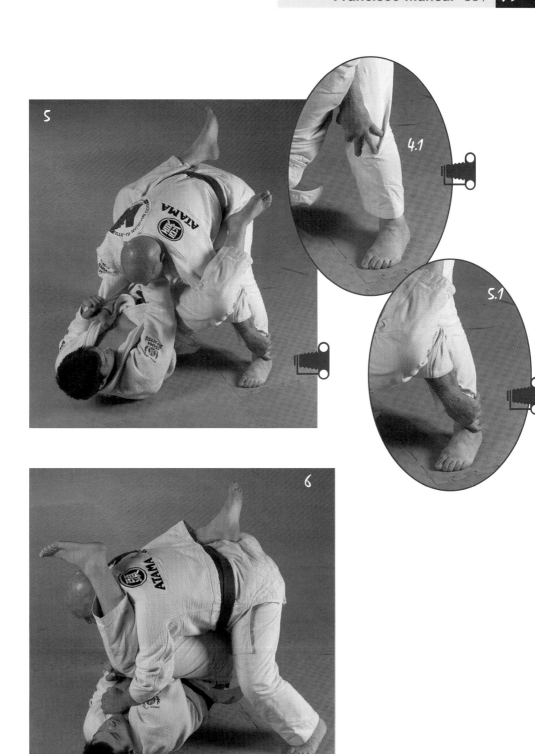

• **4ª Posição em pé na guarda** • 4th Standing guard position • **4ª Posición de pie en la guardia** • **4. Fußposition in der Deckung** • **4ᵉ Position debout dans la garde** • **4ª Posizione in piedi nella guardia**

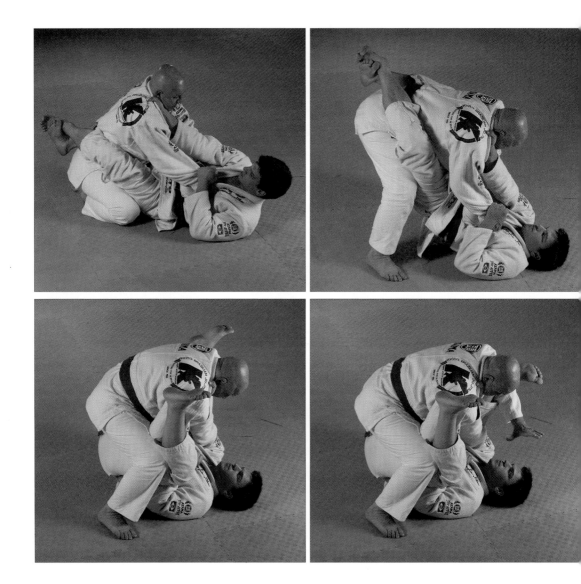

XI

Montadas • Aplicação
Mounts • Application
Montadas • Aplicación
Reiterstellung • Anwendungen
Montées • Application
Montadas • Applicazione

- **1ª Montada na 1ª Imobilizaçâo** • 1st Mount in the 1st immobilization
- **1ª Montada en la 1ª inmovilización** • **1. Reiterstellung und 1. Immobilisierung**
- **1er Montée dans la 1er immobilisation** • **1ª Montada nella 1ª immobilizzazione**

- **2ª Montada na 1ª Imobilizaçâo** • 2nd Mount in the 1st immobilization
- **2ª Montada en la 1ª inmovilización**
- **2. Reiterstellung und 1. Immobilisierung • 2ᵉ Montée dans la 1ᵉʳ immobilisation • 2ª Montada nella 1ª immobilizzazione**

- **3ª Montada na 1ª Imobilizaçâo** • 3rd Mount in the 1st immobilization
- **3ª Montada en la 1ª inmovilización** • **3. Reiterstellung und 1. Immobilisierung** • **3ᵉ Montée dans la 1ᵉʳ immobilisation** • **3ª Montada nella 1ª immobilizzazione**

- **1ª Montada na 3ª Imobilizaçâo** • 1st Mount in the 3st immobilization
- **1ª Montada en la 3ª inmovilización** • **1. Reiterstellung und 1. Immobilisierung**
- **1ᵉʳ Montée dans la 3ᵉ immobilisation** • **1ª Montada nella 1ª immobilizzazione**

- **2ª Montada na 3ª Imobilizaçâo** • 2nd Mount in the 3th immobilization • **2ª Montada en la 3ª inmovilización** • **2. Reiterstellung und 3. Immobilisierung** • **2ᵉ Montée dans la 3ᵉ immobilisation** • **2ª Montada nella 3ª immobilizzazione**

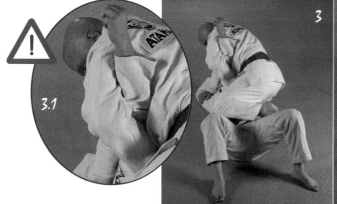

- **1ª Montada na 4ª Imobilizaçâo** • 1rd Mount in the 4th immobilization
- **1ª Montada en la 4ª inmovilización** • **1. Reiterstellung und**
4. Immobilisierung • **1ᵉʳ Montée dans la 4ᵉ immobilisation** • **1ª Montada nella 4ª immobilizzazione**

- **2ª Montada na 4ª Imobilização**
- 2nd Mount in the 4th immobilization
- **2ª Montada en la 4ª inmovilización**
- **2. Reiterstellung und 4. Immobilisierung**
- **2ᵉ Montée dans la 4ᵉ immobilisation**
- **3ª Montada nella 4ª immobilizzazione**

- **3ª Montada na 4ª Imobilizaçâo** • 3rd Mount in the 4th immobilization
- **3ª Montada en la 4ª inmovilización** • **3. Reiterstellung und 4. Immobilisierung** • **3ᵉ Montée dans la 4ᵉ immobilisation** • **3ª Montada nella 4ª immobilizzazione**

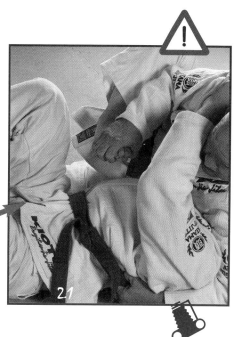

XII

Joelho na barriga
Knee on the stomack
Rodilla en la barriga
Knie im magen
Genou sur le ventre
Ginocchio sulla pancia

- **1ª Posição de joelho na barriga** • 1st Knee position on the stomach
- **1ª Posición de rodilla en la barriga** • **1. Position: Knie im Magen**
- **1ᵉʳ Position de genou sur le ventre** • **1ª Posizione in ginocchio sulla pancia**

- **2ª Posição de joelho na barriga** • 2nd Knee position on the stomach • **2ª Posición de rodilla en la barriga** • **2. Position: Knie im Magen** • **2ᵉ Position de genou sur le ventre** • **2ª Posizione in ginocchio sulla pancia**

- **3ª Posição de joelho na barriga** • 3rd Knee position on the stomach
- **3ª Posición de rodilla en la barriga** • **3. Position: Knie im Magen**
- **3ᵉ Position de genou sur le ventre** • **3ª Posizione in ginocchio sulla pancia**

XIII

Reposição de Guarda na Passagem
e Giro na passagem de Guarda
Replacement of guard in pass
and turn in guard pass
Reposición de Guardia en la Pasada
y Giro en la pasada de Guardia
Wiedereinnahme der Deckung bei Befreiung
und Befreiung der Deckung
Reposition de Garde dans le passage et
pivotement dans le passage de Garde
Riposizionamento della Guardia nel Passaggio
e Giro nel passaggio di Guardia

• **1ª Reposição da Guarda na passagem** • 1st Replacement of guard in pass • **1ª Reposición de la Guardia en la pasada** • **1. Wiedereinnahme der Deckung bei Befreiung** • **1ᵉʳ Retour à la position de Garde dans le passage** • **1° Riposizionamento della Guardia nel passaggio**

• **2ª Reposição da Guarda na passagem** • 2nd Replacement of guard in pass • **2ª Reposición de la Guardia en la pasada** • **2. Wiedereinnahme der Deckung bei Befreiung** • **2ᵉ Retour à la position de Garde dans le passage** • **2° Riposizionamento della Guardia nel passaggio**

• **1º Giro na passagem da Guarda** • 1st Turn in guard pass • **1º Giro en la pasada de la Guardia** • **1. Befreiung von der Deckung**
• **1er Pivotement dans le passage de la Garde** • **1º Giro nel passaggio della Guardia**

• **2º Giro na passagem da Guarda** • 2nd Turn in guard pass • **2º Giro en la pasada de la Guardia** • **2. Befreiung von der Deckung** • **2ᵉ Pivotement dans le passage de la Garde** • **2º Giro nel passaggio della Guardia**

XIV

• **1ª Gravata pelas costas** • 1st Tie from the back • **1ª Corbata por la espalda** • **1. Krawatte im Rücken** • **1ᵉʳ Cravate dans le dos** • **1ª Cravatta alle spalle**

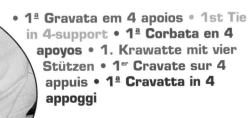

• **1ª Gravata em 4 apoios** • 1st Tie in 4-support • **1ª Corbata en 4 apoyos** • **1. Krawatte mit vier Stützen** • **1ᵉʳ Cravate sur 4 appuis** • **1ª Cravatta in 4 appoggi**

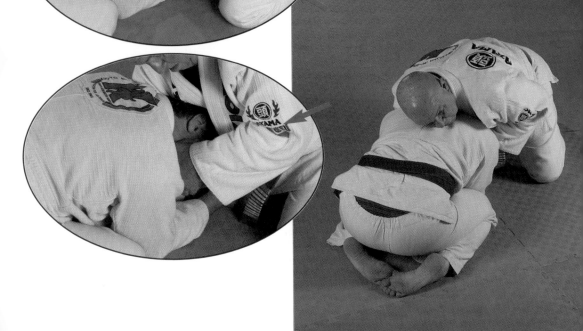

- **1ª Gravata na guarda** • 1st Tie in guard • **1ª Corbata en la guardia**
- **1. Krawatte in der Deckung** • **1er Cravate dans la garde**
- **1ª Cravatta nella guardia**

- **1ª Gravata montado** • 1st Mounted tie • **1ª Corbata montado**
- **1. Krawatte sitzend** • **1er Cravate "monté"** • **1ª Cravatta montada**

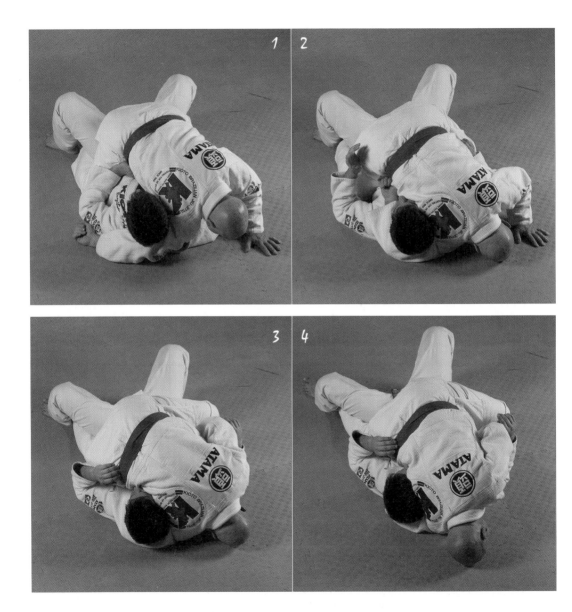

- **1ª Gravata em pé** • 1st Standing tie • **1ª Corbata de pie**
- **1. Krawatte im Stand** • **1ᵉʳ Cravate debout** • **1ª Cravatta in piedi**

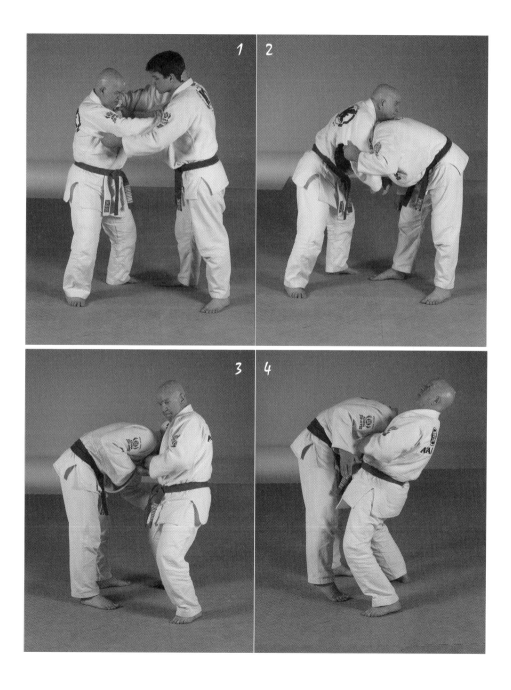

XV

Quedas
Takedowns
Caídas
Würfe
Chutes
Cadute

• Osoto Gari

• **O Goshi**

- **Ippon Seoi nage**

XVI

Passagem para as Costas em Pé
Standing pass to back
Pasada a la espalda de pie
Im Stand in den Rücken gelangen
Passage au dos debout
Passaggi alla schiena in piedi

• **1ª Passagem para as costas em pé com queda** • 1st Standing pass to back with fall • **1ª Pasada a la espalda de pie con caída** • **1. In den Rücken gehen im Stand, mit Wurf** • **1ᵉʳ Passage au dos debout avec chute** • **1° Passaggio alla schiena in piedi con caduta**

• **2ª Passagem para as costas em pé com queda** • 2nd Standing pass to back with fall • **2ª Pasada a la espalda de pie con caída** • **2. In den Rücken gehen im Stand, mit Wurf** • **2ᵉ Passage au dos debout avec chute** • **2° Passata alla schiena in piedi con caduta**

• **3ª Passagem para as costas em pé com queda** • 3rd Standing pass to back with fall • **3ª Pasada a la espalda de pie con caída • 3. In den Rücken gehen im Stand, mit Wurf • 3ᵉʳ Passage au dos debout avec chute • 3° Passaggio alla schiena in piedi con caduta**

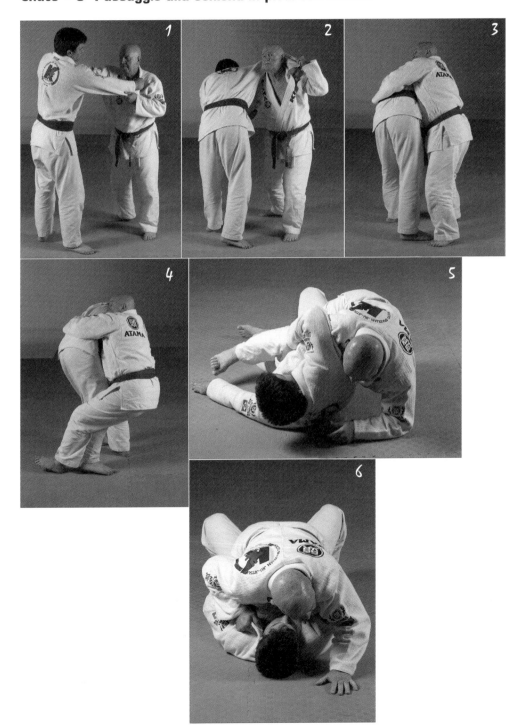

XVII

Imobilizações • Defesas
Immobilization • Defenses
Inmovilizaciones • Defensas
Verteidigende • Immobilisierungen
Immobilisations • Défenses
Immobilizzazioni • Difese

- **1ª Defesa da 1ª Osaikomi** • **1st Defense of the 1st Osaikomi**
- **1ª Defensa de la 1ª Osaikomi** • **1. Verteidigung des 1. Osaikomi**
- **1er Défense de la 1er Osaikomi** • **1ª Difesa della 1ª Osaikomi**

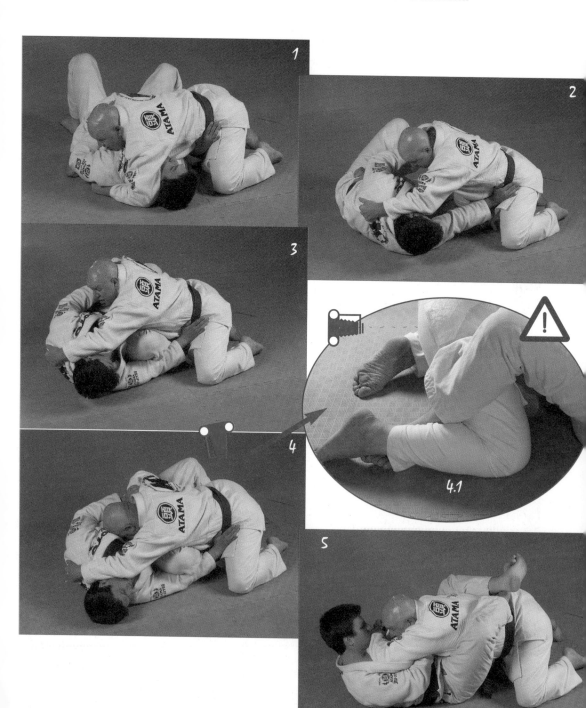

- **2ª Defesa da 1ª Osaikomi** • 2nd Defense of the 1st Osaikomi
- **2ª Defensa de la 1ª Osaikomi** • **2. Verteidigung des 1. Osaikomi**
- **2ᵉ Défense de la 1ᵉʳ Osaikomi** • **2ª Difesa della 1ª Osaikomi**

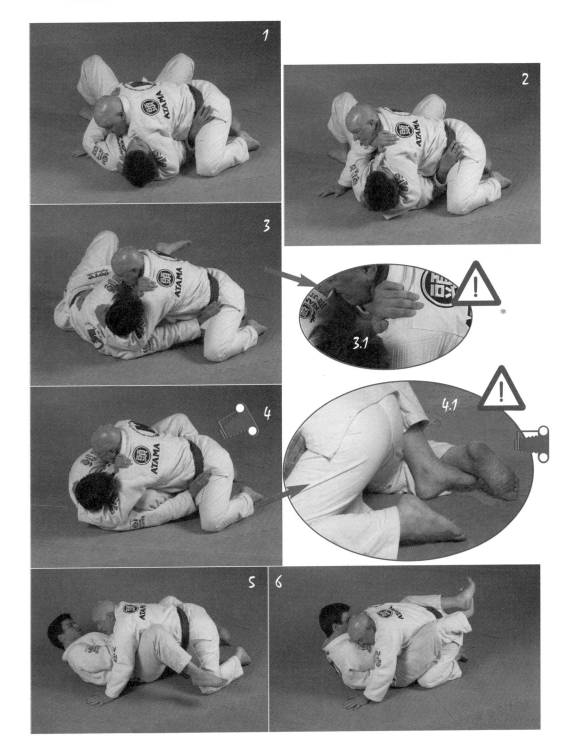

- **3ª Defesa da 1ª Osaikomi** • 3rd Defense of the 1st Osaikomi
- **3ª Defensa de la 1ª Osaikomi** • **3. Verteidigung des 1. Osaikomi**
- **3ᵉ Défense de la 1ᵉʳ Osaikomi** • **3ª Difesa della 1ª Osaikomi**

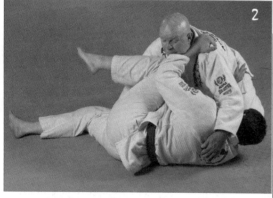

- **4ª Defesa da 1ª Osaikomi** • 4th Defense of the 1st Osaikomi
- **4ª Defensa de la 1ª Osaikomi** • **4. Verteidigung des 1. Osaikomi**
- **4ᵉ Défense de la 1ᵉʳ Osaikomi** • **5ª Difesa della 1ª Osaikomi**

- **5ª Defesa da 1ª Osaikomi** • 5st Defense of the 1st Osaikomi
- **5ª Defensa de la 1ª Osaikomi** • 5. Verteidigung des 1. Osaikomi
- **5ª Défense de la 1ᵉʳ Osaikomi** • **5ª Difesa della 1ª Osaikomi**

- **1ª Defesa da 2ª Osaikomi** • 1ft Defense of the 2nd Osaikomi
- **1ª Defensa de la 2ª Osaikomi** • **1. Verteidigung des 2. Osaikomi**
- **1ᵉʳ Défense de la 2ᵉ Osaikomi** • **1ª Difesa della 2ª Osaikomi**

- **2ª Defesa da 2ª Osaikomi** • 2nd Defense of the 2nd Osaikomi
- **2ª Defensa de la 2ª Osaikomi** • **2. Verteidigung des 2. Osaikomi**
- **2ᵉ Défense de la 2ᵉ Osaikomi** • **2ª Difesa della 2ª Osaikomi**

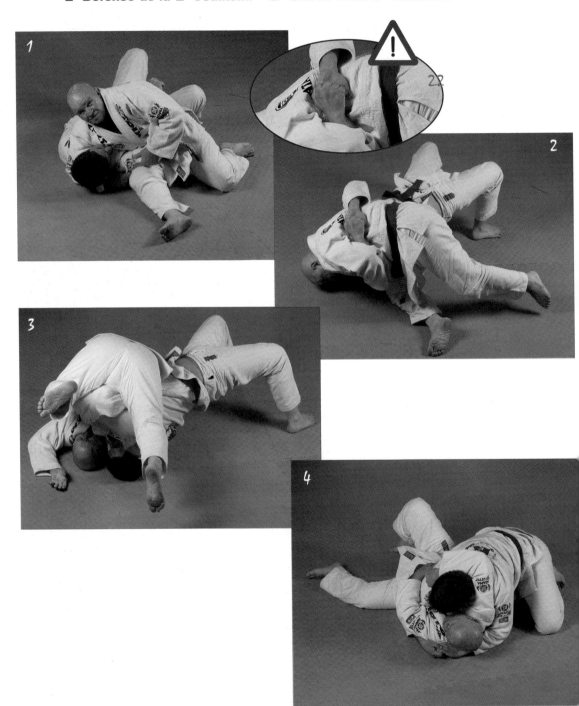

- **3ª Defesa da 2ª Osaikomi** • 3rd Defense of the 2nd Osaikomi
- **3ª Defensa de la 2ª Osaikomi** • **3. Verteidigung des 2. Osaikomi**
- **3ᵉ Défense de la 2ᵉ Osaikomi** • **3ª Difesa della 2ª Osaikomi**

- **4ª Defesa da 2ª Osaikomi** • 4st Defense of the 3rd Osaikomi
- **4ª Defensa de la 2ª Osaikomi** • **4. Verteidigung des 2. Osaikomi**
- **4ᵉ Défense de la 2ᵉ Osaikomi** • **4ª Difesa della 2ª Osaikomi**

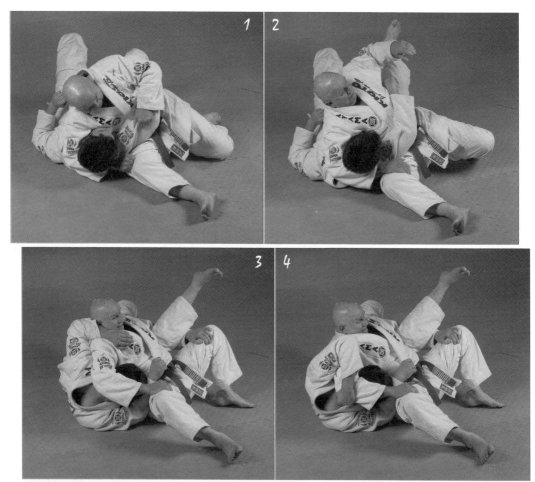

- **1ª Defesa da 3ª Osaikomi** • 1rt Defense of the 3rd Osaikomi
- **1ª Defensa de la 3ª Osaikomi** • **1. Verteidigung des 3. Osaikomi**
- **1er Défense de la 3e Osaikomi** • **1ª Difesa della 3ª Osaikomi**

- **2ª Defesa da 3ª Osaikomi** • 2nd Defense of the 3rd Osaikomi
- **2ª Defensa de la 3ª Osaikomi** • **2. Verteidigung des 3. Osaikomi**
- **2ᵉ Défense de la 3ᵉ Osaikomi** • **2ª Difesa della 3ª Osaikomi**

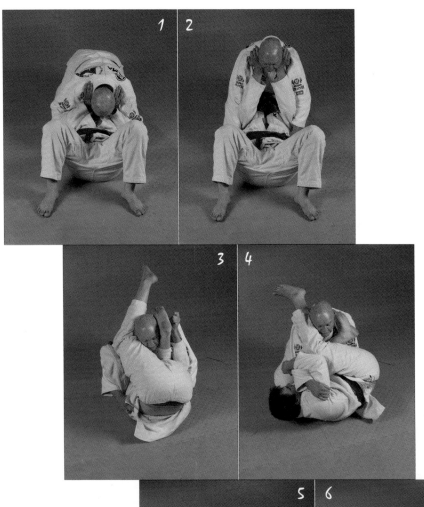

- **3ª Defesa da 3ª Osaikomi** • 3rd Defense of the 3rd Osaikomi
- **3ª Defensa de la 3ª Osaikomi** • **3. Verteidigung des 3. Osaikomi**
- **3ᵉ Défense de la 3ᵉ Osaikomi** • **3ª Difesa della 3ª Osaikomi**

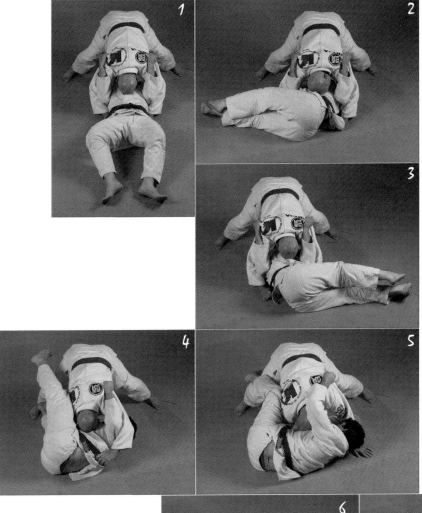

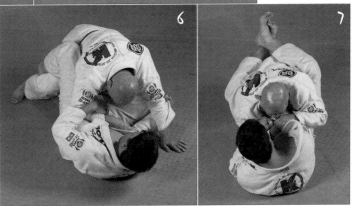

XVIII

Controle em Guarda e controle Montado
Control in Guard and Mounted control
Control en Guardia y control Montado
Kontrolle in Deckung und Reiterstellung
Contrôle en Garde et contrôle Monté
Controllo in Guardia e controllo in Montada

- **1º Controle da Montada**
- 1st Control of mount
- **1º Control de la Montada**
- **1. Kontrolle in der Reiterstellung**
- **1ᵉʳ Contrôle de la Montée**
- **1º Controllo della Montada**

- **2º Controle da Montada**
- 2nd Control of mount
- **2º Control de la Montada**
- **2. Kontrolle in der Reiterstellung**
- **2ᵉ Contrôle de la Montée**
- **2º Controllo della Montada**

- **3º Controle da Montada**
- 3rd Control of mount
- **3º Control de la Montada**
- **3. Kontrolle in der Reiterstellung**
- **3ᵉ Contrôle de la Montée**
- **3º Controllo della Montada**

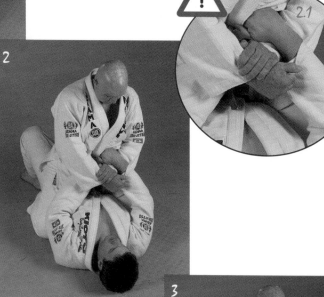

- **4º Controle da Montada** • 4th Control of mount • **4º Control de la Montada 4. Kontrolle in der Reiterstellung** • **4ᵉ Contrôle de la Montée** • **4º Controllo della Montada**

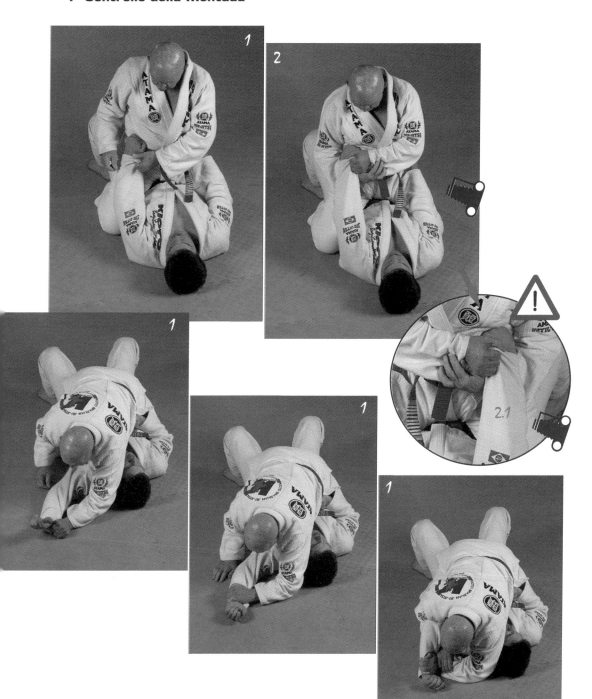

• **1º Controle em Guarda** • 1st Control in guard • **1º Control en Guardia** • **1. Kontrolle in der Deckung** • **1ᵉʳ Contrôle en garde** • **1º Controllo in Guardia**

• **2º Controle em Guarda** • 2nd Control in guard • **2º Control en Guardia** • **2. Kontrolle in der Deckung** • **2ᵉ Contrôle en garde** • **2º Controllo in Guardia**

• **3º Controle em Guarda** • 3rd Control in guard • **3º Control en Guardia** • **3. Kontrolle in der Deckung** • **3ᵉ Contrôle en garde** • **3º Controllo in Guardia**

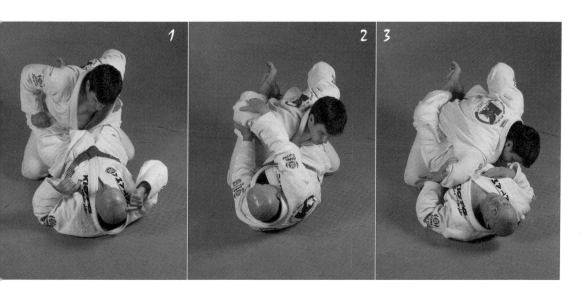

• **4º Controle em Guarda** • 4th Control in guard • **4º Control en Guardia** • **4. Kontrolle in der Deckung** • **4ᵉ Contrôle en garde** • **4º Controllo in Guardia**

XIX

Triângulos e Armlocks
Triangles and Arm-locks
Triángulos y Armlocks
Dreiecke und Armhebel
Triangles et Armlocks
Triangoli ed Armlocks

• **1º Triângulo em Guarda** • **1st Triangle in Guard** • **1º Triángulo en Guardia** • **1. Dreieck in der Deckung** • **1ᵉʳ Triangle en Garde** • **1º Triangolo in Guardia**

• **2º Triângulo em Guarda** • 2nd Triangle in guard • **2º Triángulo en Guardia** • **2. Dreieck in der Deckung** • **2ᵉ Triangle en Garde** • **2º Triangolo in Guardia**

• **1º Triângulo em 4 apoios** • 1st Triangle in 4-support • **1º Triángulo en 4 apoyos** • **1. Dreieck mit den 4. Stützen** • **1ᵉʳ Triangle sur 4 appuis** • **1º Triangolo in 4 appoggi**

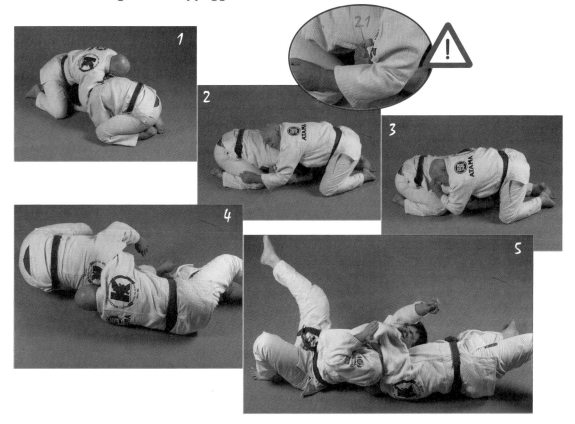

- **1º Armlock Montado** • 1st Mounted arm-lock • **1º Armlock Montado**
- **1. Armhebel sitzend** • **1ᵉʳ Triangle sur 4 appuis** • **1º Armlock in Montada**

- **2º Armlock Montado** • 2nd Mounted arm-lock • **2º Armlock Montado**
- **2. Armhebel sitzend** • **2ᵉ Armlock Monté** • **2º Armlock Montada**

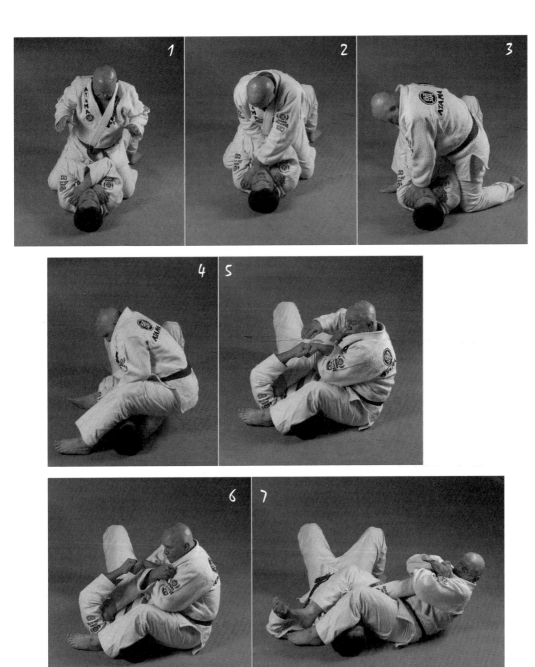

- **1º Armlock no 1º Osaikomi** • **1st Arm-lock in the 1st Osaikomi**
- **1º Armlock en el 1º Osaikomi** • **1. Armhebel im 1. Osaikomi**
- **1er Armlock dans le 1er Osaikomi** • **1º Armlock nel 1º Osaikomi**

• **1º Armlock em guarda** • 1st Arm-lock in guard • **1º Armlock en guardia** • **1. Armhebel in Deckung** • **1ᵉʳ Armlock en garde** • **1º Armlock in guardia**

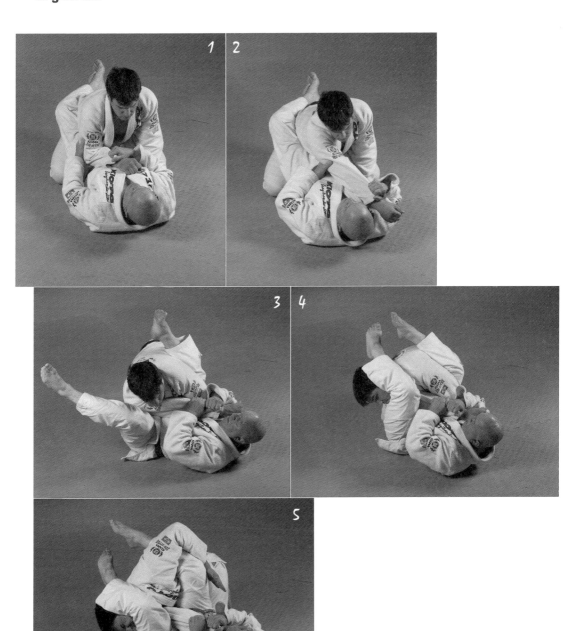

• **2º Armlock em guarda** • 2nd Arm-lock in guard • **2º Armlock en guardia** • **2. Armhebel in Deckung** • **2ᵉ Armlock en garde** • **2º Armlock in guardia**

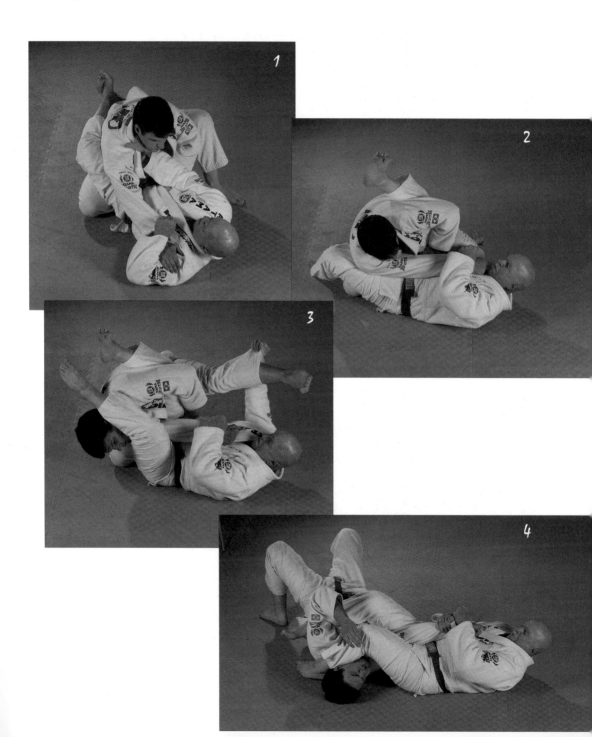

- 1º **Armlock no 3º Osaikomi** • 1st Arm-lock in the 3rd Osaikomi
- 1º **Armlock en el 3º Osaikomi** • **1. Armhebel im 3. Osaikomi**
- 1er **Armlock dans le 3e Osaikomi** • 1º **Armlock nel 3° Osaikomi**

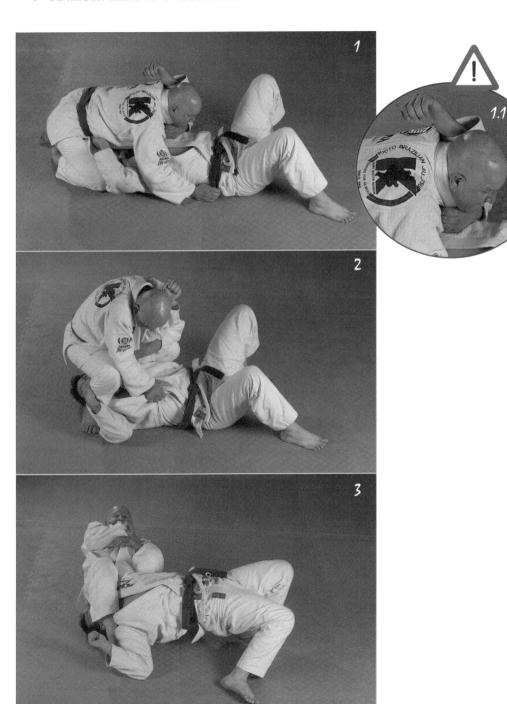

- **1º Armlock em 4 apoios** • 1st Arm-lock in 4-supports • **1º Armlock en 4 apoyos** • **1. Armhebel im 4 Stützen** • **1ᵉʳ Armlock sur 4 appuis**
- **1º Armlock in 4 appoggi**

ÍNDICE

INDEX

INDICE

INDIZE

INDEX

INDICE

Index